D0843013

# Focus on
# School

A Reference Handbook

# TEENAGE PERSPECTIVES

# Focus on
# School

## A Reference Handbook

Beverly A. Haley

LA
229
.H24
1990

WITHDRAWN

SAINT LOUIS UNIVERSITY
0 2 3

ABC-CLIO

Santa Barbara, California
Oxford, England

© 1990 by ABC-CLIO, Inc.

All rights reserved. No part of this publication may be reproduced, stored in a retrieval system, or transmitted, in any form or by any means, electronic, mechanical, photocopying, recording, or otherwise, except for the inclusion of brief quotations in a review, without prior permission in writing from the publishers.

**Library of Congress Cataloging-in-Publication Data**

Haley, Beverly A., 1929–
    Focus on school : a reference handbook / Beverly A. Haley.
      p.   cm. — (Teenage perspectives)
    Includes bibliographical references.
    1. High school students—United States. 2. High school students—
United States—Life skills guides.  I. Title.  II. Series.
    LA229.H24  1990     373.18'0973—dc20     89-18637

ISBN 0-87436-099-4 (alk. paper)

97 96 95 94 93 92 91 90      10 9 8 7 6 5 4 3 2 1

ABC-CLIO, Inc.
130 Cremona Drive, P.O. Box 1911
Santa Barbara, California 93116-1911

Clio Press Ltd.
55 St. Thomas' Street
Oxford, OX1 1JG, England

This book is Smyth-sewn and printed on acid-free paper ∞ .
Manufactured in the United States of America

*For Mom and Dad*

# Contents

# Chapter 6: Looking to the Future, 165

# Foreword

An old Chinese curse goes, "May you live in exciting times." Today's young people have grown up under such a curse—or blessing. They live in a world that is undergoing dramatic changes on every level—social, political, scientific, environmental, technological. At the same time, while still in school, they are dealing with serious issues. Making choices and confronting dilemmas that previous generations never dreamed of.

Technology, especially telecommunications and computers, has made it possible for young people to know a great deal about their world and what goes on in it, at least on a surface level. They have access to incredible amounts of information, yet much of that information seems irrelevant to their daily lives. When it comes to grappling with the issues that actually touch them, they may have a tough time finding out what they need to know.

The Teenage Perspectives series is designed to give young people access to information on the topics that are closest to their lives or that deeply concern them—topics like families, school, health, sexuality, and drug abuse. Having knowledge about these issues can make it easier to understand and cope with them, and to make appropriate and beneficial choices. The books can be used as tools for researching school assignments, or for finding out about topics of personal concern. Adults who are working with young people, such as teachers, counselors, librarians, and parents, will also find these books useful. Many of the references cited can be used for planning information or discussion sessions with adults as well as young people.

Ruth K. J. Cline
Series Editor

# Preface

School—who needs it? That's how some teenagers feel these days.

These teenagers unfortunately have a negative view of what is happening to them at school. They are unable to see the connection between their experiences at school and their lives outside of it. Yet there are other teenagers who have a different attitude about the time at school. By their performance in the classrooms, their participation in extracurricular activities, and their contributions to their communities, these teenagers show that school is enhancing their lives and preparing them for the future.

Going to school, it seems, is an experience that affects individuals differently. But the things that happen (or fail to happen) during those days and years in a school setting can, on the one hand, lead one teenager toward a clear and meaningful path for life but, on the other, leave a classmate feeling confused, incompetent, frustrated, frightened, bitter, or hurt. What has gone right for one along the way and wrong for the other?

This volume takes a close look at why things can go right in school and what to do so they won't go wrong. It examines the school experience to identify what teenagers need to know and understand, so that their schooling will be meaningful and productive. It gives useful information about the educational process and an understanding of how the school years can strongly influence what will happen in the future. The material in this volume will also serve as a resource to help readers understand and focus the direction of their lives—or the lives of others.

Chapter 1: "Understanding the School's Role" discusses the history, purpose, structure, and nature of school in the United States; alternatives to public schools; and study-travel possibilities.

Chapter 2: "Understanding the Student's Role" explores why school is important, what young people need to know now and in the future, how to plan a course of study, how to find good teachers and classes, and how to decide about cocurricular and extracurricular activities.

Chapter 3: "Focusing for Success" looks at the nature of success, the student's responsibilities, how to keep grades in perspective, how to make homework work effectively, how to take tests, how to get along with teachers, and how to overcome barriers to success.

Chapter 4: "Learning and Growing Outside of School" presents ideas on how students can prepare for and enhance what they learn at school by participating in sports and outdoor activities, informal social and organized group activities, the world of work, and cultural activities.

Chapter 5: "Getting Help" offers ways to handle the toughest problems students may encounter during the school years—the places to go and the people to ask for help, and how to find options, depending on whether a student's problem is personal, caused by a situation at school, or due to trouble at home.

Chapter 6: "Looking to the Future" explores the many options and choices available after high school graduation— how to choose a focus, and then how to focus on that choice; how to decide whether or not to get more or new vocational training and/or go to college; how to choose a school and write letters of inquiry or application, complete application forms, and have a successful interview. Tips for getting financial help are also included.

Following each chapter is a suggested list of print and nonprint resources for readers who want to explore certain topics in greater detail. Resource categories include fiction, nonfiction, film and video, organizations, and hotlines.

The fiction titles can lead students to experience, through story, situations that can help them solve their own problems, explore new ideas and lifestyles, have an exciting adventure that tests courage and intelligence, achieve difficult goals, and learn to understand why people behave the way they do.

The nonfiction titles can help students who want to learn more information on their own or who need to complete a report or research assignment. Bibliographies included in nonfiction books can in turn lead to further research and exploration of a topic.

Film and video bring visual and auditory pleasure to learning and can enrich or, in some cases, replace print materials. Individuals can locate resources listed in this volume in libraries and bookstores by looking in the card catalogs and by using the computer terminals; and the reference sections in libraries have indexes of films, filmstrips, and videos that include full ordering information. Computers connect many libraries and bookstores today to others across the nation, making virtually any document, published or not, available to people who live even in remote areas. Books, films, and videos are loaned by mail. Copies of requested magazine articles and unpublished print materials can be sent through interlibrary loan as well. Libraries also have reference indexes of organizations or associations for people who are interested in becoming a part of a particular interest group. These groups are also good sources for information on their special areas.

Historical societies and museums are additional rich resources for books, pamphlets, films, displays, and artifacts about schools. Government, business, and industry frequently offer free and inexpensive materials for educational purposes. Information about how to write to such sources can also be found in the reference section of the library or by going to such places that might be located nearby. A major objective of this volume is to present the many resources teenagers can access that will help them achieve success in their school experiences. With so much information available, finding out who can help with a particular problem and where to get help is part of successful learning in today's world.

Beverly A. Haley

# CHAPTER 1

# Understanding the School's Role

Teach these boys and girls nothing but Facts. Facts alone are wanted in life.

> Charles Dickens, *Hard Times*
> (New York: A Signet Classic,
> 1961 [1854]), 11.

Written more than a century ago, these lines from Charles Dickens's novel might just as easily have appeared in this morning's newspaper. In the novel, Mr. Gradgrind allows no human or emotional element to muddy his clear objective to teach "nothing but Facts" to the children in his school. So ardently does the teacher adhere to this philosophy that instead of calling upon the students by name to recite or to answer questions, he calls on "Boy Number One" or "Girl Number Three."

Many students in some of today's large urban schools— and even those in smaller schools—may feel at least part of the time as if they were simply numbers like Gradgrind's pupils, rather than individuals with human needs and desires. And the followers of an educational philosophy similar to Mr. Gradgrind's that children be taught "nothing but Facts" are a vocal element today. They are the ones who call out for more academic courses, more solids, and who could easily have been quoted in a newspaper this morning.

Another article or editorial or interview in that same newspaper, however, might very well argue from an opposite point of view, suggesting a quite different approach to what schools should do and how they should do it. It might, for example, point to the need for schools to teach the values that institutions like the family, the church, and the community were once expected to instill in children.

> He has learned nothing except to toady to those he feels are superior.
> William Saroyan, *The Human Comedy*
> (New York: Dell Publishing,
> 1973 [1943]), 58.

Miss Hicks, who teaches ancient history in Saroyan's novel, suggests that young people learn—or fail to learn—moral values and qualities of character in school. Guiding the development of students' characters continues to be one of the functions some segments of society want today's schools to perform.

---

The purpose of school and how students are taught intertwines with history and how people lead their lives. As society changes, schools adjust themselves to accommodate the changes and to prepare young people to fit into the society in which they will live. But the question arises: Does society influence the nature of school, or does the nature of school shape the direction of society? The question can be argued either way, but in either case, both the tradition and structure of twentieth-century schools tend for the most part to be difficult and slow to change.

One underlying purpose for the existence of school, though, remains unchanged: to pass on to young people the skills, guiding principles, and cultural heritage they need to become successful adults. A complementary purpose, not so easily measured, is to arm students with the necessary skills they need to continue learning after they complete their formal schooling.

Conflict about which skills, which principles, and which heritage rages and subsides within the schools—and among the general public. Controversy about censorship ebbs and flows. And disagreements about how the teaching should be done creates a variety of educational philosophies, each with its followers. The challenge to hold onto some kind of consistency in education—so that teachers and students don't get confused—while celebrating the richness of diversity sometimes proves overwhelming. But the educational process moves along, and the uniquely American concept of providing the opportunity for formal schooling to everyone remains at the heart of the purpose of education in the United States.

## Knowledge and Credentials

Knowledge will forever govern ignorance; and a people who mean to be their own governors must arm themselves with the power knowledge gives.
James Madison, quoted by Wendell Pierce
in "Education's Evolving Role,"
in *A Nation of Learners* (Washington, DC:
U.S. Government Printing Office, 1976), 126.

James Madison warned that Americans must impart knowledge to young people, and that young people must take on the responsibility of gaining knowledge or the new democracy could neither survive nor thrive. That fundamental purpose for the existence of schools is sometimes forgotten when people compete to acquire knowledge in order to gain personal wealth and power.

Although one purpose of the public schools in a democracy is to do away with elitism, circumstances have not always contributed toward the ideal of equal opportunity for all. In the nation's early years, blacks and girls, who often helped run the house and cared for younger children, customarily did not go to school. Other problems included a lack in the number and the quality of schools and the need for young people to help the family on the farm or in the family business. And although the first colleges were established as early as 1636 (Harvard) and 1693 (William and Mary), only those young people from more privileged circumstances could take advantage of a higher education.

Not until the 1960s did legislation of the mid-1950s begin to desegregate schools' racial populations. The U.S. Supreme Court's *Brown v. Board of Education* decision on May 17, 1954, stating that "separate educational facilities [for blacks] are inherently unequal" (Farmer, 143), brought long-awaited, long-fought-for rights to people in the black population. What had only been implied in the Constitution now was directly stated. In order to achieve that purpose, students were taken from neighborhood schools and bused, sometimes great distances, so that every school in the district would show a certain racial balance. Protests, riots, and furor raged, resulting in injuries, deaths, and imprisonments in a number of instances.

But despite busing and other efforts, there are still vast differences in the quality and the number of options available to students from school to school, and the goal of equal educational opportunity for all seems virtually unattainable.

Meanwhile, battles for other kinds of equal opportunity brought about progress for the physically and mentally handicapped, for non–English-speaking immigrants (particularly when they arrive in large numbers), for those of lower socioeconomic classes, for women, and for illiterate adults. Such events as the 1970 White House Conference on Children and the Bicentennial Year of the Child have focused on the right of every young person to learn. In the case of adults, the community colleges, the Adult Basic Education movement, and recent amnesty laws have helped alleviate the problem of adult illiteracy and made it possible for many to become self-sufficient.

The replacement of industrialism with the age of technology has forced institutions of higher learning to open classes— indeed, to create specific courses—for nontraditional (older than 24 years of age) students. The notion that school is only for the young has shattered, replaced with the knowledge that everyone must periodically or continuously learn and/or retrain.

In the early days of the nation, the governing fathers' worries over competition with nations overseas drove them to keep up with what was happening there in politics and economics as well as in religion and in the arts and sciences. But they wanted to do more than merely keep up with the Old World; they wanted to surpass it. And they were eager to establish a tradition and a culture that would be uniquely American.

From the beginning, a controversy arose, too, about the primary purpose of schools: Should they "transmit an inherited body of culture" or should they instead focus on training young people in "useful skills" (Handlin, 3)? As the nation began to develop economically and thrust forward into the Industrial Revolution, fewer young people learned their trades or vocations from parents or as apprentices to other adults. More and more families moved off the farms and into the cities. The purpose of school and what was to be taught expanded. During the nation's colonial period, schools attempted to prevent people from relapsing into barbarism by focusing on the study of the Bible in its Hebrew, Greek, and Latin translations. In the mid-eighteenth century—even before the Revolution— schools added readings from a largely European heritage along with the study of mathematics.

When President Woodrow Wilson signed the Smith-Hughes Act on February 23, 1917, the legislation broke the long tradition of excluding vocational training (normally acquired in workshops or on farms) from the classroom curriculum. This government action opened the way to meet the nation's growing need for skilled workers brought on by the Industrial Revolution (Rumpf, 90). With production shifting from home to factory and from handcraft to power-driven machinery, the responsibility for vocational training shifted to the schools.

Thus schools began training young people in vocational and homemaking skills. As a result, people became confused about the purpose of schools, particularly high schools and colleges. Should they be institutions for job training or for transmitting a cultural heritage to enrich the human mind and enhance social well-being? This confusion over purpose, which still exists today, endangers the clear fulfillment of either or both goals.

As the influence and teachings of church and community on young people lost power—for a variety of reasons, including the weakening and spreading out of family and community structure, the rising population, and the migration to the cities—society looked to the schools to teach socialization skills, courtesy and manners, personal hygiene, and moral behavior. Child labor and mandatory school age laws were passed to protect vulnerable young people against physical and mental oppression in the factories and to ensure that they had the opportunity for a formal education. With each succeeding generation, more people were staying in school longer and more high school graduates continued on with some form of occupational training or academic schooling following graduation.

During this century schools also began transporting students who lived beyond a certain distance to and from school, providing midday meals, teaching driver education, and incorporating into their programs interschool competition in sports, music, and other activities. They became, at least from one point of view, both a day-care service and a way to keep teenagers out of the adult job market, once again meeting the changing needs of society. Today, though, at least half of all high school students hold part-time jobs—low-paying or menial jobs that many adults don't want. In what may yet be the greatest revolution in the way schools function, the needs of a modern high-tech, information-based society are again forcing educators to redirect the focus of the purpose and function of school.

Saul Bass, a filmmaker of short but thought-provoking films often used in high school classrooms, has said that schools now have a special challenge to meet. Students today, he contends, must "develop a flexible, open, ruminative, discursive, creative ability to look at a condition and find a relationship to it in a very individual and special way. If students don't have this quality, they will grow up in their world with a set of skills that they cannot use, with information that is outdated before they have the opportunity to use it" (Sohn, 13).

Throughout the history of school in the United States, those who run the schools have faced problems and obstacles, not the least of which is money. Not enough money for buildings, equipment, materials, supplemental services, instructors, and administrators has been blamed for not giving all of the nation's young people the best possible formal schooling. Unequal funding, largely because funding is primarily done locally, has meant that some schools have plenty of money to purchase the best, the most, and the latest, whereas schools in poorer districts have suffered from inadequately equipped schools and sometimes less qualified staff members.

While the democratic ideal requires the underpinnings of an educated society, one problem in schooling the masses is that of discipline. Discipline, in this case, suggests maintaining order to create an environment where 20 to 35 students, on the average, can focus their attention on learning. Just as what is taught and how it's taught reflect the values of society during a particular time, so too does the way schools address the issue of discipline change with the times.

Even when a master teacher (at any given time in the history of schools) plans and teaches lessons in a way that motivates young people to learn, there are times when situations and behavior require some system of punishment and reward. Schools use punishment and reward systems for several reasons: to maintain order, to ensure attendance, and to ensure that lessons are completed. Some teachers punish people who either are slow to learn or who are brighter or know more than the teacher. Some students may feel they're punished for belonging to a different ethnic group, for being male or female, for living in the "wrong" section of the city, or because an older brother or sister created problems in the school. While consistency and fairness should underlie any system of reward and punishment, most people hold biases that may be difficult to overcome.

One system of reward and punishment—that of awarding numerical or letter grades for performance in learning—is discussed in Chapter 3. A line from the old song "School Days" noting that reading and writing and arithmetic were "taught to the tune of a hickory stick" suggests the prevalent use of physical punishment. Physical punishment and humiliation in front of others lingered well into the nineteenth century and even into this century. Two examples of this type of punishment were " 'sitting on the wall' (squatting in a sitting position with only the back against the wall for balance)" and " 'holding nails into the floor' (stooping for hours)" (Appleby, 41). The hickory stick of the song "School Days" suggests the use of a stick or whip to punish students. But the effects of verbal abuse, coming from a teacher's sharp, sarcastic, or thoughtless comment, could be more devastating and long-lasting. Such a tongue-lashing could strip a young person of dignity and self-respect.

The first state to legislate protection for children from abuse was New York. In 1875 that state designated child abuse as a criminal offense. A full century later in 1974 an act of the U.S. Congress established a National Center on Child Abuse. Francis Roberts wrote in *Parents* magazine in 1988 that at that time only nine states had outlawed corporal punishment in the public schools, with New York still being one of the leaders in this reform. Ironically, Roberts editorializes, nearly every state says it's illegal for an adult to hit another adult. Roberts labels physical punishment as an "unnecessary and outmoded" way to control young people, adding that such punishment "may develop life-long hostility toward authority," a factor "that can contribute to later violent behavior." Roberts also notes that such treatment of youth by adults can create fear in other students that has the effect of inhibiting learning.

Despite countless problems and controversies, though, the fact remains that U.S. schools have managed to accomplish to a surprising degree the democratic purpose of giving many people the opportunity to learn and become successful in life. No other nation's public school system has ever been able to succeed as well in educating as many people—both citizens and immigrants—as has the one in the United States.

# The Structure of School

Even though the odor of chalkdust and the scrape of chalk remain part of today's classrooms, a variety of tools came into common use during the 1970s that suit the age of technology— television sets and tape recorders, computers and printers, hand-held calculators, and overhead projectors—increasing the scope of teaching and learning methods immeasurably.

The one-room schoolhouse of two centuries ago with its wood benches, potbellied stove, shelves at various heights to fit various sizes of students, dunce stool and cap, and schoolmaster's or mistress's whip no longer exists. In those former years, few teenagers were among the students and those who were there came only if they weren't needed at home to work. And they were mostly boys. Girls could learn everything they needed to know from their mothers and be useful to them at the same time. Even when teenage girls began going to school, they were often restricted to taking classes in home economics. The few teenage girls who did learn enough academic knowledge to pass the state teacher's exam rarely continued their formal education and became schoolmistresses instead.

Nearly two centuries ago, school days tended to be long and tedious with the boys arriving at 7:00 A.M. in spring and autumn, 8:00 A.M. in winter, and not leaving—except for an hour to walk home and back for lunch—until 5:00 P.M. (Selden, 8). Pupils memorized their lessons and recited them aloud. The noise level rose higher and higher as the boys simultaneously recited different lessons.

If those teenagers of long ago could catch a glimpse of a modern classroom—its books in bright bindings with full color illustrations, the gymnasiums and cafeterias and music rooms, the spacious outdoor grounds and parking lots lined with rows of students' cars—they'd think they'd landed on a different planet. Yet in some basic ways, schools then and now aren't very different.

Whereas each school, just as each person, has its own personality with its own set of strengths and weaknesses, schools in general—both as buildings and as institutions—also share certain characteristics:

1. The school building is constructed with several floors and/or several wings, each designated for a different grade level or subject area. The floors and wings of the building are usually divided into separate classrooms (permanent or flexible) where a teacher instructs a series of between 5 and 7 classes daily, each made up of approximately 20–35 students.

2. Usually students are separated into grade levels according to chronological age and academic advancement. The number of students in a school can vary widely, from as few as 10 to 4,000 or more.

3. The school year and the school days are divided into units of time, such as 4 quarters or 2 semesters a year and 6 or 7 periods each day for classes, lunch, and special activities.

4. Teachers are expected to teach, and students to learn, a body of knowledge and skills that follows a district curriculum guide. Textbooks and other materials are selected, approved, and adopted by the district. Parents and interested citizens have an opportunity to examine the materials before they're adopted.

5. Rules (such as those for behavior, attendance, dress) are established to keep order and to maintain a certain amount of equality and fairness for students. Rules also contribute to students' safety and well-being, though often students think that rules restrict their freedom or are unnecessary—and sometimes that's true.

6. Levels of school organization follow a prescribed hierarchy:

> The United States Department of Education (makes laws, provides some funding)
>
> The state department of education (makes laws for state schools, provides a large amount of funds)
>
> The local district's board of education, superintendent, principals of each school, assistant administrators at all levels (govern policies and practices for the local school district)
>
> Accountability committees and parent organizations
>
> Teachers (who have their own hierarchy including master teachers, department chairpersons, specialty teachers, classroom teachers, teacher's aides, and student aides) and counselors
>
> Support personnel, such as nurses, mental health and social workers, secretaries, cooks and dieticians, bus drivers, grounds and building custodians

Student government

Taxpayers

These levels of a hierarchy—which has taken over two centuries to evolve—add up to a cadre of people working together to continue an instructional system whose purpose it is to prepare young people for adult life.

In his book *A Place Called School*, John Goodlad described how he and a team of assistants studied a number of different kinds of schools over a period of years. Goodlad and his team examined the particular structure of each school, any special procedures unique to that school, and how the total approach to administration and teaching affected how well students learned. The results of the study indicated that the strongest influence on the effectiveness of a school is people. Each school had a distinctly different approach to education from the others; and while a common structure placed each inside the definition of "school," they varied widely in size, style, and student achievement. The primary element that has remained stable in all schools, both through time and from the most traditional to the most experimental classroom today, is the teacher.

## What Makes a Good School?

> There was much gossip and idle talk among the students; but no one in this school laughed at learning. . . . I felt myself floating and gliding and flying through this school. . . .
>
> Chaim Potok, *Davita's Harp* (New York:
> A Fawcett Crest Book, 1986 [1985]), 300.

As Goodlad's study points out, each school develops a distinctive personality. That personality suits the learning style of some students more than it does other students who learn in other ways. This is the kind of experience the high school student in Potok's novel described in comparing her reaction to the school to which she recently transferred, with her feelings about her previous school.

Unquestionably, some schools create a richer learning environment for their students than do other schools, and a number of studies have pointed out those qualities shared by effective schools. A list compiled of such findings includes these common elements:

The school principal is a strong, active leader.

Staff members share a firm commitment to continually improve the school.

Adults in the school demonstrate high expectations for positive student behavior, for their students' capacity to learn, and for the students' desire to learn.

The school defines clear goals and makes carefully considered plans and decisions about courses, content, and activities for the students.

The environment is safe, clean, and orderly.

The school's absentee and suspension rates are low.

Staff and students demonstrate mutual respect and a sharing of values, goals, and planning.

The staff is committed to the teaching and learning of basic skills.

Curriculum, textbooks, and supplementary materials give students a wide spectrum of ideas and knowledge from which to choose what they will value and incorporate in their personal beliefs and actions.

Students develop skills and master a body of knowledge that they can then apply to specific situations.

The school provides continuous evaluation of progress and constructive feedback to its students.

Students learn to learn independently as well as cooperatively in the school.

Students develop and practice a strong sense of social responsibility.

The school receives active support from the superintendent, parents, and community.

The school enjoys a wide reputation for excellence.

The principal sets the tone in a school. Teachers and students respond to the principal's styles and tend to rise (or stoop) in relation to the leader's cues for doing what is expected (or not expected) of them. A good principal is a strong role model.

Although the principal sets a climate for the school, it is the teacher who sets the tone inside each classroom. Since students spend most of their school days in classrooms, it is their teachers who have the greatest impact on the quality of learning students achieve. A teacher who has command of the subject matter and who also understands how to work with and motivate people to learn makes a good teacher. Teachers who themselves are strongly motivated, who enjoy life and learning, who are willing to work hard and to persevere—in short, the sparkling, dynamic teachers—become the master teachers in any school.

But teachers who lack confidence in their knowledge and in themselves create confusion and fear in the classroom. As a result, the teaching/learning process can become severely crippled. As Loren Eisely wrote, "The educator can be the withholder as well as the giver of life" (Sohn, xi).

## Evaluating a School's Effectiveness

To evaluate its effectiveness, those who are interested can take a look around a school—at its classrooms, corridors, cafeteria, gym, and music room. Does the school look uncared for with litter in the halls, graffiti on the walls, and thoughtless behavior of people toward one another?

What kinds of cocurricular or extracurricular activities does the school offer and support? Do regular visiting lecturers and performers enrich the students' learning? Is there a student government? If so, how much real power does it have in decisions about what goes on in the school? Do students feel that teachers and administrators listen and respond appropriately? What are the school's rules and regulations? How are they enforced? Do they support the well-being of students? What types of special services are offered—such as speech therapists, school psychologists or social workers, tutoring, and guidance in planning schedules and for life after graduation? Are parents involved in decisions that affect school policy, curriculum, and activities? How much and what kind of communication network operates among school administrators, teachers, students, parents, the community?

# Alternatives to Public Schools

While a majority of students in the United States attend public schools, there are alternatives. And the number of those alternatives is increasing for a number of reasons: criticism of the public schools; belief by some that religion and religious teachings should be integral to the curriculum; the fact that not every person fits comfortably into the traditional school setting; government options that would give parents the means to send their children to the schools of their choice without paying tuition.

Critics of the voucher or choice system say it will breed elitism and destroy the original idea that public schools are integral to democracy. Supporters of such systems say that competition will raise the quality of schools and that the ability to choose is important for citizens' rights. Indeed, a number of states already have choice systems. Minnesota has embarked on the largest commitment to the concept of choice, with an increasing number of its districts being required to offer parents the choice of schools for their children as well as giving high school students the right to take one or more courses in local colleges. The state of Vermont prides itself on a tradition of choice in school. A number of districts in Massachusetts allow their residents choices, as do several in Nebraska, Arkansas, Iowa, and a growing number of other states.

Public school systems today are devising choices of their own within the system. A couple of examples of this type of restructuring are the schools-within-a-school and the magnet schools. In the schools-within-a-school plan, students with different interests and talents or learning styles can choose from among several programs available in one school. A district using the magnet school system assigns each campus in the district a different focus; for example, one campus takes a traditional approach, the second designs its curriculum around vocational training, another concentrates on math and sciences, while yet another takes the arts and humanities for its core approach. Parents and students together decide which school best suits the young person's learning style and interests, then apply for acceptance to the one of their choice. Some states have established state schools, for example, for students with special math interest and ability or for others whose talents are in the performing arts. Those whose homes are distant from the school of their choice live near or on school grounds during the academic year. And the year-round school is yet another experiment in increasing the level and quality of learning in some districts as an alternative to the traditional September through June academic year.

Even when schools are structured alike within a given district or in neighboring districts, they differ in size, in the strengths and weaknesses of certain programs, and in the type of student population. If someone thinks another school suits his or her learning style better, then it could well be worth the time and effort to request a transfer. If the school a student wants is in a neighboring district, a waiver of tuition might be granted if good reasons for the change are presented to the board of education. Some students live away from home with a relative or close family friend or as a boarder in order to attend a school of their preference. This alternative is not a new one. In earlier generations, farm children who wanted to attend high school often lived with townspeople during the school months.

Some public school districts offer an alternative high school as another option. While the stereotypical perception of the alternative school is that it's for troublemakers, the fact is that young people choose alternative school for a variety of reasons: some because they feel like outcasts in the regular school, some because they like to set their own learning goals and have a closer relationship with teachers, and others because they are bored in the traditional school. Such alternative schools can be very different from one another in size, approach to teaching, and curriculum, but frequently they require students to accept responsibility for their learning and set realistic goals for themselves.

Another type of public school that is gaining popularity in various places across the nation is the "learning by doing" school, similar to the alternative program in Colorado's Jefferson County school district. (This approach is similar to the "progressive education" that was popular during the 1920s, '30s, and '40s.) This alternative program focuses on developing quality and diversity. Keeping enrollment at no more than 200, the school's curriculum includes many field trips, community learning experiences, community service, and a culminating project called the Walkabout where students are asked to use their skills in real-life settings (Gregory and Smith, Chapter 6).

## PRIVATE SCHOOLS

By far the largest majority of private schools have been the parochial schools. And the greatest number of parochial schools are Catholic. But there are also other private schools, military schools, and special programs for travel and study.

Private schools cost money. Parochial schools offer scholarships, sometimes work-study, or parent-work to help with the cost. More exclusive private schools can be very expensive. As a result, their students generally have wealthy families although these schools offer scholarships as well. College preparatory schools present a strong academic program to those students who plan to attend highly selective colleges and universities.

Some of the differences between public and private schools are that private schools can reject whomever they choose or can tell students who aren't fitting in that they will no longer accept them. Generally, private schools require close involvement from all parents, and in many cases the class sizes are smaller. In contrast to the current credentials required of public school teachers (with some new exceptions), teachers in private schools may range from having very few credentials to having the very best, depending upon the school. Many private schools require students to wear uniforms; some are for young women or for young men only; and some present a military program with strict codes of discipline and order. In parochial schools, either the textbooks include religious study or special classes teach religious beliefs. Often private schools don't offer as many extracurricular activities as do public schools, but they may provide a different type and range from those in a public school.

Many educators believe that the presence of both public and private schools in the United States is healthy. Each can look at what the other is doing and then take a closer look at themselves for ways to make what they do better. Educator John Goodlad once commented that the role of private schools is "largely one of setting an educational pace, breaking new ground, providing exemplary models for public schools to follow" (*What Schools Are For*, 25).

## HOME-SCHOOLING AS A CHOICE

Another option that has grown in popularity in recent years is that of home-schooling. Such a choice needs careful thought. Home-schooling demands commitment, hard work, networking with others, positive family relationships, continual awareness, and money. A family considering home-schooling needs to check on the legal aspects involved in the state where they live.

For some young people, home-schooling works; for others, it's a disaster. But for whatever reasons, the number of home-schoolers is on the rise. According to the United States Department of Education figures, the number of registered home-schoolers increased from 15,000 home-taught children in 1970 to more than a quarter-million in 1988. The actual count is probably higher since many home-school families don't officially register. A September 1988 news release said 260,000 youth were being schooled at home, adding that this number is twice that reported for 1985.

Those who make the choice to teach their children at home represent a wide range of backgrounds. For example, Mike Dwyer, president of the Colorado Home Educators Association, said that "We've got people from fundamentalist Christians to atheists and New Age people, and outside home-schooling, they're on opposite ends of the spectrum but home education unites them" (*The Sunday Denver Post*, 22 May 1988, 11).

Home-schoolers in a geographical area often organize to share resources, plan group activities, and discuss common problems. State and national groups also help provide resources and sharing. People who choose to school at home tend to explore the community as a rich resource—for example, they use libraries, museums, individuals with particular talents and knowledge, and community organizations.

Just as in the traditional school setting, home-schoolers take different approaches to the teaching-learning process, ranging from a formal schedule adhered to on a daily basis to an informal, learn-as-we-do style. The main point is that parents take primary responsibility for providing their children's schooling. One California couple (who have also published a book on how to home-school), Micki and J. David Colfax, have taught three sons. Each has gone on to be admitted to Harvard University—and to perform well there. Mrs. Colfax said she thinks "public, especially high-school-age children, are mostly a holding operation." Both the Colfaxes are trained teachers (*The Denver Post*, 4 September 1988, 17A).

## Exchange Study and Travel

Students can also take advantage of travel or exchange study, either in their own country or in other countries. A long list of approved programs provides just about any type and length of such an experience to students interested in learning more about other ways of life and at the same time adding to their formal schooling. For those who aren't ready to leave home for such an experience but still would like to learn about how others think and live, the option to host a student from another part of the country or from another land might be the best choice.

The Council on Standards for International Educational Travel produces an annual pamphlet published by the United States Information Agency that lists approved programs for students interested in this kind of study and experience. The guide features a programs-at-a-glance centerfold chart with more detailed descriptions under category headings. Special kinds of programs like Presidential Classroom, Up With People, People to People High School, Student Ambassador Program, and School Exchange Service are also included.

Regardless of a school's size, appearance, geographical location, or its approach to preparing young people to grow into productive adults who take joy in their work and in life, school is a two-way process between those who teach and those who learn. In a healthy environment, the roles of teaching and of learning switch back and forth easily and at will.

## REFERENCES

Appleby, Bruce C. "Is Adolescent Literature in its Adolescence?" *The ALAN Review*, National Council of Teachers of English, Fall 1989, 40–45.

Colfax, J. David, and Micki Colfax. Associated Press article. *The Denver Post*, 4 September 1988: 17A.

Dickens, Charles. *Hard Times*. New York: A Signet Classic, 1961 [1854].

Farmer, James. "Toward Educational Opportunity." *A Nation of Learners*. Washington, DC: Department of Health, Education and Welfare, U.S. Government Printing Office, 1976. 139–145.

Goodlad, John, et al. *A Place Called School*. New York: McGraw-Hill, 1984.

———. *What Schools Are For*. Bloomington, IN: Phi Delta Kappa Educational Foundation, 1979.

Gregory, Thomas B., and Gerald R. Smith. *High Schools as Communities: The Small School Reconsidered*. Bloomington, IN: Phi Delta Kappa, 1987. Chapter 6, 119–122.

Handlin, Oscar. "Education and the American Society." *A Nation of Learners*. Washington, DC: Department of Health, Education and Welfare, U.S. Government Printing Office, 1976. 3–7.

Madison, James, quoted by Wendell Pierce. "Education's Evolving Role." *A Nation of Learners*. Washington, DC: Department of Health, Education and Welfare, U.S. Government Printing Office, 1976. 125–131.

Potok, Chaim. *Davita's Harp*. New York: A Fawcett Crest Book, 1986 [1985].

Roberts, Francis. "Corporal Punishment in the Schools." *Parents,* May 1988, 41.

Rumpf, Edwin L. "The Voc Ed Breakthrough." *A Nation of Learners.* Washington, DC: Department of Health, Education and Welfare, U.S. Government Printing Office, 1976. 90–91.

Saroyan, William. *The Human Comedy.* New York: Dell Publishing, 1973 [1943].

Selden, Judith. "Master Dove's One-Room School." *A Nation of Learners.* Washington, DC: Department of Health, Education and Welfare, U.S. Government Printing Office, 1976. 8–9.

Sohn, David. Film: *The Creative Eye.* Dayton, OH: George A. Pflaum, 1970.

# Resources

The following list of resources can serve as a starting point for those who are interested in making further explorations into the history, purpose, structure, and nature of school; about alteratives to public schools; and/or about study-travel experiences. Students may want to request media help.

## Fiction

Conroy, Pat. **The Lords of Discipline.** Boston, MA: Houghton Mifflin, 1980. 499p.

The story is set in the late sixties at the time of the Vietnam War and takes place in a boys' four-year military school in the South. The narrator, who is himself a product of that schooling, describes how at first he tries to conform to the strict demands and rituals required of the students but ends by breaking the rules and disdaining the military approach to schooling.

Cormier, Robert. **Beyond the Chocolate War.** New York: Dell Publishing, 1985. 278p.

In his sequel to *The Chocolate War*, Cormier again shows how life in an all-boys Catholic high school breeds contempt for rules, despite the boys' fear of punishment for breaking those rules. A bright but cruel boy organizes a gang, creating a hierarchy of student authority within the adult authority. As a result, school and learning become secondary and the teenage dictatorship is even more frightening to students than that imposed by adults. One of the characters plans suicide, another determines to get revenge, and several others attempt to break away from the tight grip of the gang.

Dickens, Charles. **Hard Times.** New York: A Signet Classic, 1961 [1854]. 292p.

This classic gives young readers today some perspective on how school, students, and teachers have changed in more than a century, yet shows them what has remained the same. The proprietor of an experimental private school in an English manufacturing town, Thomas Gradgrind, builds his school on his fanaticism for facts. When the results destroy his own children as human beings and end their chances for happiness, Gradgrind admits at last that the human element cannot be left out of an education for the young.

Kerr, M. E. **Is That You, Miss Blue?** New York: Dell Publishing, 1976 [1975]. 172p.

Life in a private girls school for Flanders Brown means she has to get used to a new world of rules, restrictions, daily church services—and teachers' idiosyncrasies and cliques formed by girls who shut her out. While she gets into more trouble at school, the problems there keep her mind off the messy family situation she left at home.

Kiesel, Stanley. **Skinny Malinky Leads the War for Kidness.** New York: Lodestar, 1984. 163p.

This fantastic and funny adventure gives a student's-eye view of the public school system, beginning with Mr. Foreclosure's plan to turn all remaining kids (from the book preceding this sequel) into goody-goody Young People. Skinny Malinky leads the war to foil this evil scheme.

Knowles, John. **A Separate Peace.** New York: Bantam Books, 1968 [1959]. 196p.

The narrator, an adult who returns to Devon School for boys where he spent his prep school years, looks back on those pre–World War II boarding school experiences with bitter-sweet force and dual vision. Gene (the narrator) focuses on his competitive experiences—both in and out of the classroom—with Phineas. In the teenagers' interaction, the forces of good and evil become intricately intertwined. This classic novel was made into a film.

Potok, Chaim. **The Chosen.** Greenwich, CT: Fawcett Publications, 1967. 271p.

The friendship between two boys of Jewish faith, one Orthodox and the other Reformed, evolves against the backdrop of the differences and similarities in their respective home and school lives. Each boy sees advantages and disadvantages in the family and education of the other. And each learns from the other as they share the pains and joys of growing up as they study and set personal goals for the future. A movie version maintains the novel's spirit.

Saroyan, William. **The Human Comedy.** New York: Dell Publishing, 1973 [1943]. 192p.

In this episodic World War II era story, a young teenager, Homer Macauley, tries to take the place of his dead father and his older brother who is away at war. Homer lies about his age to get an after-school job to help pay for the care of his mother, sister, and younger brother. Homer tries to excel at school and in track even though he's weary from overwork and sometimes feels prejudice at school from classmates of higher social classes. A teacher, Miss Hicks, gives her students instruction not only in ancient history but also in matters of importance in life—fairness, honesty, the value of knowing great minds and thoughts, and loyalty.

Taylor, Mildred D. **Let the Circle Be Unbroken.** New York: Bantam Books, 1983 [1981]. 339p.

In her sequel to the well-known *Roll of Thunder, Hear My Cry*, Mildred Taylor continues the history of teenager Cassie Logan and her family, blacks who have managed to get a farm of their own and must struggle to keep it. Cassie's parents, strong believers in the value of education, insist that the children attend a school for blacks only (they're not allowed to go to the school for white children), do their homework, and learn. Mrs. Logan is one of the teachers and sets an example for her own and the neighbors' children. The people in the book face the overwhelming obstacle that the poor and the blacks have in being denied access to the better school.

Weesner, Theodore. **The Car Thief.** New York: Dell Publishing, 1972 [1967]. 352p.

Weesner's story is of Alex Housman, an inner-city student who lives alone with his father, a hard-working man who works night shift at the nearby factory and sleeps most of the day. Lonely and unable to explain his problems to a concerned teacher or to a female classmate he's attracted to (both of whom would have helped him), Alex is constantly torn between studying and doing what's right (where he fears he can't succeed) and stealing cars and getting into trouble with the law (where he succeeds very well). The novel helps readers assess and understand similar choices they or their peers may confront in their need to succeed in school and in life.

# Nonfiction

Boyer, Ernest. **High School.** New York: Harper and Row, 1983. 256p.

This report by the Carnegie Foundation for the Advancement of Teaching sets forth the results of the committee members' study. The report describes in detail a number of selected high schools throughout the nation using criteria the committee believed would give a picture of the state of education for high school students as well as a description of what the students themselves are like.

Colfax, David and Micki. **Homeschooling for Excellence.** New York: Warner Books, 1987. 142p.

The authors, whose own three home-schooled children have won admission to Harvard University, identify resources and methods for teaching children at home.

Council on Standards for International Educational Travel (CSIET). **Advisory List of International Educational Travel and Exchange Programs, 1988.** Reston, VA: CSIET, 1987. 104p.

Council members evaluate, recommend, and provide standards for educational travel programs as a service to schools and to prospective international high school students and their parents and advisors. Programs are monitored in a way that assures participants a certain level of quality in a travel-study experience. The handbook is revised annually to include programs for the current year.

Some schools as well as youth groups like 4-H and the Boy Scouts and the Girl Scouts also offer various types of exchange experiences or sharing that provide rich learning opportunities for young people.

Edinger, Lois V., Paul L. Houts, and Dorothy V. Meyer, eds. **Education in the 80s: Curricular Challenges.** Washington, DC: National Education Association, 1981. 188p.

This collection of essays by educators with different backgrounds and points of view is intended to stimulate dialogue among all those concerned with education and its future. Selected chapters will be of special interest to students. The book's five parts include: Societal Expectations for Public Education, Teachers and Students of the 80s, The School Program: The Nature of the Curriculum for the 80s, The Politicalization of Education, and The Unfinished Agenda.

Glasser, William, M.D. **Schools Without Failure.** New York: Harper and Row, 1975 [1969]. 228p.

Noted author/psychiatrist Glasser uses cases and examples as the core of this book about the problem of too many student failures in schools today. He proposes dramatic changes in educational philosophy, recommending commitments for involvement, relevance, and thinking to reverse the growing trend of failure.

Goodlad, John. **A Place Called School.** New York: McGraw Hill, 1983. 396p, bibliography.

Educator/author Goodlad with a team of colleagues spent years studying, participating in, and evaluating a selected variety of schools. The results they gathered were then used to draw conclusions about what works and what doesn't work in the teaching-learning process in the school setting.

————. **What Schools Are For.** Bloomington, IN: Phi Delta Kappa Educational Foundation, 1979. 127p and bibliography.

Goodlad's thesis is that schools spend too much time training and not enough time educating teenagers. He discusses definitions and functions of high schools, both social and educational, and then proposes ways to improve the schools we have and to strive toward a society that continues to educate.

Haertel, Edward H., Thomas James, and Henry M. Levin, eds. **Comparing Public & Private Schools, Vol. 2: School Achievement.** Philadelphia, PA: Falmer Press, 1987. 148p.

This volume contains studies comparing the academic achievement of public and private (primarily Catholic) schools, based on data from the High School and Beyond survey of the United States Education Department.

**The Handbook of Private Schools,** 69th ed. Boston: Porter Sargent Publishers, 1988. 1,478p.

This handbook provides a statistical and descriptive listing of 1,788 private schools in the United States.

Havighurst, Robert J., and Bernice L. Neugarten. **Society and Education,** 3rd ed. Boston: Allyn & Bacon, Inc., 1968 [1967]. 507p, bibliography and suggestions for further reading at end of each chapter.

This comprehensive work discusses school as a social structure in America, as a socializing agency, and as a member of the community. Noting the changing patterns of work and leisure, expanded functions of the federal government in education, the problem of unemployed and out-of-school youth, the authors call for new ideas in education and in teaching to meet the needs these changes create.

Leonard, George B. **Education and Ecstasy.** New York: Dell Publishing, 1968. 239p.

Education writer and consultant George Leonard discusses the problems and potential of schools, treating topics such as the nature of education, the human potential, the chain of learning, teachers and schools, schools and the future, and the uses of ecstasy. Leonard celebrates the joy of learning and of living and suggests ways schools can make such a vision a reality. The book is especially noted for its readability.

Lieberman, Myron. **Beyond Public Education.** New York: Praeger Publishers, 1986. 237p, two appendixes.

The author includes chapters on family choice proposals, the benefits of a private school, characteristics of private schools, and entrepreneurial schools. Appendix B contains a copy of the proposed California Voucher Initiative.

Mitchell, William, with Charles Paul Conn. **The Power of Positive Students.** New York: William Morrow, 1985. 191p.

The authors promote a program for increasing school effectiveness by teaching students positive self-esteem.

**A Nation of Learners.** Department of Health, Education and Welfare. Washington, DC: U.S. Government Printing Office, 1976. 184p.

Published in the nation's bicentennial year, the collection of essays on all aspects of school in the United States provides an overview of the evolution of school as it is today, many insights into the changes and the traditions, and a look at what schools of the future may be.

Postman, Neil. **Amusing Ourselves to Death.** New York: Viking Penguin Inc., 1985. 180p.

Postman contends that more education of young people is going on in front of the television set than from the front of the classroom. Using this definition of education as a metaphor, Postman warns about the need to be aware of the "curriculum" young people are choosing and what the sources of information, values, lifestyle, and goals are telling them. Postman says they should also be aware of what motivations lie behind that curriculum and just how it's training their minds and characters.

Postman, Neil, and Charles Weingartner. **The School Book.** New York: A Delta Book, Dell Publishing, 1975 [1973]. 297p, index, resource list.

Postman and Weingartner narrow the definition of school to its bare bones, and describe briefly and with insight its history, structure, and purpose. They talk about why the public, once seemingly accepting of schools, is now complaining. They include an informative section on the language of school, provide short biographies of and comments about leaders in school criticism and reform, and give an account of significant court decisions that have affected how schools function.

Powell, Arthur G., Eleanor Farrar, and David K. Cohen. **The Shopping Mall High School: Winners and Losers in the Educational Marketplace.** Boston, MA: Houghton Mifflin, 1986. 360p.

The authors compare today's high schools to shopping malls where everything is available, everybody is there, and there's something for everyone. The student as consumer can get as much or as little as he or she chooses—so it's important to know how to shop, what to buy, and why to buy it.

Richman, Howard and Susan. **The Three R's at Home.** Kittaning, PA, 1988. 230p.

Designed for parents who are considering teaching their own children or are already engaged in home-schooling, this volume suggests approaches to teaching reading, writing, and mathematics.

Some periodicals devoted to what's currently happening in schools and education today include *Education Week,*

*Education Digest, Phi Delta Kappan, NASSP Bulletin,* and many others that can be found in the education section of most libraries.

# Nonprint Materials

### Education
*Type:*     3/4″ or 1/2″ video, color
*Length:*   15 min.
*Source:*   Agency for Instructional Technology
            Box A
            Bloomington, IN 47402
*Date:*     1983

The film examines humanity's shared commitment to education. It shows that for the children of the Tarahumara Indians this means commuting to distant boarding schools and learning Spanish, while the Baoule children of West Africa learn French because that is the language used in schools. The Japanese experience a rigorous education program designed to help them succeed in a global society. (From the Across the Cultures Series.)

### Education by Choice
*Type:*     16mm film, 3/4″ or 1/2″ video, color
*Length:*   29 min.
*Source:*   Films, Inc.
            5547 North Ravenswood Avenue
            Chicago, IL 60640
*Date:*     1975

The film illustrates the education by choice program offered by a high school in Quincy, Illinois. It reviews the development of the seven separate programs and some of the implications for secondary education of the future.

### Education—The Realities
*Type:*     2″ video, b/w
*Length:*   30 min.

*Source:*  Great Plains Instructional TV Library
University of Nebraska
P.O. Box 8066924
Lincoln, NE 68501

Depicting the realities of the education system, the videotape examines the public's indifference; the low estate, status, and competence of teachers; and the burdens placed on education. It explains that these can only be alleviated by a renovation of policies and practices. (Broadcast quality, from the Communications and Education Series, no. 20.)

**Education in America—A Series**
*Type:*  16mm film, 3/4" or 1/2" video
*Length:*  16 min. each, 3 in series
*Source:*  Coronet Instructional Films
108 Wilmot Road
Deerfield, IL 60015
*Date:*  1958

The series traces the history of education in America, from the earliest New England schools to the Supreme Court decisions of the 1950s, with the first film covering the seventeenth and eighteenth centuries, the second giving a view of the nineteenth century, and the third highlighting events of the twentieth century through the 1950s.

**Educational Directions—Where Do We Go from Here?**
*Type:*  16mm film, optical sound, color
*Length:*  27 min.
*Source:*  East Texas State University
Chapter of Phi Delta Kappa
Commerce, TX 75428
*Date:*  1977

The film analyzes the basic philosophical foundations of educational systems in the 1970s and in years past. It proposes alternatives for the future by educational philosophers such as Marshall McLuhan, John Goodlad, and Nolan Estes.

**High School**
*Type:*  16mm film, 3/4" or 1/2" video, color
*Length:*  75 min.

*Source:*     Zipporah Films
            One Richdale Avenue, Unit 4
            Cambridge, MA 02140

The film emphasizes that the school system exists not only to pass on facts but to transmit social values from one generation to another. It documents how this social conditioning occurs and shows formal and informal encounters between teachers, students, parents, and administrators through which the ideology and value of schools emerge.

**Priceless Heritage**
*Type:*       16mm film, color
*Length:*     23 min.
*Source:*     The Film Library
            Learning Resources Service
            Southern Illinois University
            Carbondale, IL 62901-6510
*Date:*       1971

Taken from Alphonse Daudet's "Last Lesson," the film is the story of the last class being taught in a small Alsatian school before the Germans take over command. Poignant, emotionalized, and patriotic, the film gives the viewer, too, the final lesson taught in French as the town officials look on. The realization of what has been lost as well as something of society's power structure and the old-fashioned methods of instruction can be realized. The story opens and closes briefly in an American school.

**Stand and Deliver**
*Type:*       Video
*Length:*     103 min.
*Cost:*       Purchase $19.98
*Title no.:*  ADWHV011805
*Source:*     Critics' Choice Video
            800 Morse Avenue
            Elk Grove Village, IL 60007
*Date:*       1988

The popular movie, now available in video, dramatizing the courageous struggle of the teacher, Jaime Escalante, who transforms tough kids in an urban California school into national math competition winners has inspired countless students to believe in themselves and to achieve in school.

# Organizations

### American Association of Christian Schools (AACS)
10195 Main Street, Suite P
P.O. Box 1088
Fairfax, VA 22030
(703) 273-6114
*Executive Director: Dr. Gerald B. Carlson*

Founded in 1972, the organization maintains teacher and administrator certification and placement services as well as a placement service and school accreditation. It sponsors sports events among Christian schools and publishes a monthly newsletter, a semiannual journal, and an annual directory and holds an annual convention/meeting.

### American Association of School Administrators (AASA)
1801 North Moore Street
Arlington, VA 22209
(703) 528-0700
*Executive Director: Richard D. Miller*

Founded in 1865, the association is "dedicated to the continuing professional and personal development of school administrators," is the founder of Educational Research Service, and could be a resource for studies and publications relating to the quality of schooling.

### Home and School Institute (HSI)
Special Project Office
1201 16th Street, NW
Washington, DC 20036
(202) 466-3633
*President: Dorothy Rich*

Founded in 1965, the institute seeks to reaffirm the educational importance of the home and community. It develops strategies for school-family, school-community, and business-family involvement; provides ways to strengthen home environment for learning; sponsors several projects; and publishes a number of items including home and school curriculum and books.

## The National Association of Secondary School Principals (NASSP)
1904 Association Drive
Reston, VA 22091
*Executive Director: Scott Thomson*

Composed primarily of secondary school principals and vice principals, the association makes studies, conducts research, appoints standing committees for a wide range of subcategories of interest, holds workshops and seminars and meetings regularly (state, regional, and national), and develops a number of publications for wide distribution including newsletters, a journal, and pamphlets and books on particular subjects of importance to secondary school administrators, counselors, and teachers that may also be of interest to students. Regular news releases make research and information widely available to the public.

## National Rural and Small Schools Consortium (NRSSC)
c/o National Rural Development Institute
Miller Hall 359
Western Washington University
Bellingham, WA 98225
*Director: Doris Helge, Ph.D.*

The consortium seeks to improve the quality of rural and small school education by establishing partnerships with rural businesses and associations. It maintains a library, compiles statistics, operates a speakers' bureau, and produces several types of publications.

## National Study of School Evaluation (NSSE)
c/o Vernon D. Pace
5201 Leesburg Pike
Falls Church, VA 22041
*Executive Director: Vernon D. Pace*

This organization conducts study and research on the problems of evaluating schools in order that standards and procedures of evaluation might be improved. It promotes continuous and progressive improvement of schools through the development and publication of evaluation instruments. It also develops appropriate materials.

# CHAPTER 2

# Understanding the Student's Role

> Growing up poor has really . . . made me take a good
> look at myself as well as at the people around me. I
> have seen so many of my family members and child-
> hood friends pass up the opportunity for an educa-
> tion and subsequently . . . witnessed their downfall.
>
> Sylvia, age 18,
> in a personal interview (April 1989).

For Sylvia, who grew up in poverty, staying in school and
doing well enough to go on to college spelled her way out of
the cycle of poverty and gave her hope for a better life. But she
had to overcome many obstacles to make that dream come
true. The first and most forbidding was that she received no
support from her family or friends. The summer before her
senior year of high school, Sylvia began living on her own and
supporting herself by taking two jobs. Because of her special
needs, she withdrew from the traditional high school and
enrolled in an alternative school since its smaller enrollment
and relaxed rules allowed her to design her own goals and plan
of study. She went to school from 8:00 A.M. until 2:00 P.M.,
reporting for her job in a meat packing plant by 2:30 P.M. to prepare her knives and other tools to begin work on the night shift
by three o'clock. She didn't get back to her small trailer again
until after midnight. Then she cleaned up and finished the
homework assigned for the next day. When spring came, she

stayed up even later writing letters of application to colleges and filling out scholarship forms. It was a grueling schedule.

People kept telling Sylvia, "You'll never make it." And there were many times when she thought the same thing, times she was so tired she didn't even care whether she made it or not. That was when she forced herself to remember her goal— to picture in her mind the life she did not want for herself, and then to picture the life she did want. The contrast between the images motivated her to keep going. Not only did she earn her high school diploma but she qualified for financial help that meant she could enter a university. The university she chose had a special program for Sylvia and others like her that would give her various kinds of help—tutoring, a support group, emotional counseling, advising, any assistance that would help her stay in school and get her degree, enabling her to seek employment as a social worker.

Charlie, another senior, was staying in school because his father forced him to. He couldn't see that school was important for him. After all, he was already a successful bull rider on the professional rodeo circuit. School was simply postponing what he really wanted to do and, as far as he could tell, not giving him a thing that even faintly resembled what could help him in his chosen career. As a bull rider he was already being accepted by adults as an adult in the world he wanted.

For Tammy, school was a place where she could meet her friends, flirt with the guys, join lots of clubs, and dream about Saturday night's party. Her parents bought her expensive clothes and a fancy sports car; the family traveled to interesting places several times a year. The academic part of school, the class-work, was "kid's stuff." What could it possibly give her that she didn't already have? She could making passing grades without too much effort and by making sure she pleased her teachers.

---

# Why School Is Important

First-generation Americans and those who are the first in their families to get a high school diploma and go on to college (like

Sylvia) value school as the way to a good life more than do students who already have the good life. School is more important for some people than for others. And school can be important in different ways to different people. But with the rapid changes taking place today people will need at least a high school diploma with additional training and education to get the skilled jobs that ensure them a decent living and work environment. Staying in school is important for a broad range of reasons.

Headmaster of Boston Latin Academy, Dr. Robert Binswanger believes that people's high school years are "an important learning period, a time to determine not only who they are and what they want to be, but how they can get there, and it's an exciting time in terms of preparing for what the world is going to be like in the 21st century" (*The Fort Morgan Times*, 11 January 1988, 3). His statement agrees, in its first portion, with psychologist Erik Erikson, who said that during the teenage years young people face the task of discovering and defining their unique identities (227–229).

For earlier generations what had to be learned at school was less complex than what people need to learn today. Learning to read, write, do arithmetic, understand some science, and master a body of knowledge that changed little from year to year was considered solid schooling. It seldom mattered whether individuals ended their schooling after the sixth, eighth, or twelfth grades unless they wanted to become doctors, engineers, lawyers, or university professors. But today's fast-changing technological world makes it imperative that people complete a high school education followed by post–high school training or education, as well as return to school periodically for retraining and reeducating, either within a given field or to enter a new one. Students like Charlie may be able to have the kind of life they want now without gaining competence in the subject matter most high schools require, but their opportunities for future change—as well as the ability to change—are limited.

The high school years enable students to extend the scope of what they have already learned. During the middle school/ junior high school years students master the basic skills of reading, writing, and computation. They are also introduced to history, the sciences, exercise and health, and the practical and fine arts. High school gives students the time and opportunity to explore their interests in greater depth or to discover interests they didn't know they had. These explorations help students define who they are, how they want to live, what they want to do with their lives, and the kinds of people they want to live and play and work with. In high school, students learn to recognize and make the most of who they are as individuals, their capabilities, their capacity for growth along with their limitations. They're learning to think of themselves in terms of where they came from, who they are now, and where they're going.

The curriculum and the activities offered in high school can strengthen the foundation of knowledge individuals need on which to build new learning.

Corporate employers Kearns and Doyle wrote that they look for "employees who are broadly and deeply educated, men and women who are 'liberally' educated." Because employers are often too busy and often lack the resources, these corporate leaders warn, they "cannot train the uneducated." (24)

But career preparation isn't the only reason to take advantage of what school offers. A broad education will also lay the necessary background for people to lead rich, satisfying lives as human beings. An education helps people understand the complexities of modern life, appreciate literature and the arts, and increase their potential for satisfying employment. School can help develop people's abilities to benefit both themselves and others. Horace Mann, who influenced education in the nineteenth century, charged the graduating seniors at Antioch College in 1859, "Be ashamed to die until you have won some victory for humanity" (Keppel, 134). That message is as valid today as it was then.

In another comment by Boston Latin Academy headmaster Binswanger, the educator observed that talented high school students already contribute to the communities where they live, saying that "I'm encouraged by the fact that they are a positive force for change and good in society" (The Fort Morgan Times, 11 January 1988, 3). High school students don't have to wait until they're adults to be forces for good in society. They can be powerful influences now—and feel good about themselves.

# What Young People Need To Know Now and in the Future

I guess a lot of people are concerned about how to
take charge of their lives and make them better.
                Terry Davis, *Vision Quest* (New York:
                    Bantam Books, 1981 [1979]), 166.

Author Terry Davis's protagonist, high school senior Louden
Swain, made the decision to take charge of his own life and
make it better by taking on both academic and athletic challenges during his school years. Whether he was aware of it or
not, when he established positive attitudes, goals, habits, and
motivations while he was young, he was setting the direction
for his adult life as well. The things people need to know now
in order to achieve success are the same ones they'll need to
know in the future.

To be prepared for the twenty-first-century world—one
probably more complex than today's—young people need to
learn information and master skills their grandparents might
never have imagined. Examining what some experts predict
people will need to know in the future can help high school
students focus their schooling today.

A glance at what's happened to work since the turn of this
century shows that in 1900 85 percent of workers were in
agriculture, most unskilled, jobs; in 1989 just 3 percent of the
workforce was in agriculture—and most of these skilled or
professional. The same sort of transformation has occurred in
manufacturing. According to Willard R. Daggett, director of
occupational education for the New York State Department
of Education, 44 percent of workers in 1989 were in the service
sector, most at unskilled jobs. Daggett predicts that by the year
2000, that figure will change to 36 percent, most of whom
will be skilled. Skill and knowledge are necessary in order for
people to get the kinds of jobs that can earn them a decent
living.

Results of a survey of classroom teachers, school administrators, media specialists, college faculty, and state and federal
officials revealed a consensus that students should master the
four Cs—"comprehension, critical thinking, communication,

and coping"—if they are to prepare themselves adequately for life in a "complex and technically oriented world" (" 'Four C's' Envisioned," 9).

Educator Herbert Kohl expands on these four Cs when he suggests that today's basics of education include that students:

> Master the ability to use language effectively and with thought
>
> Learn to understand how people behave in groups and then apply that understanding both to group problems and personal problems
>
> Understand and use their knowledge of tools and of scientific and technological ideas
>
> Think through a problem, then visualize or experiment with different solutions by using their imaginations
>
> Learn through practice to use and appreciate a variety of forms of expression
>
> Know how to learn on their own in order to get both the skills and the confidence needed to continue learning throughout life (Kohl, 110–111)

Another educator adds to these basics by saying that it's important to "learn how to learn, learn to adapt to change, learn to be versatile in different areas of vocational skills, [and] to develop a favorable position toward social responsibilities" (Cheong, 1984).

Thus a brief look at these new basics of education clearly shows that no longer is going to school a matter of reciting lists of memorized rules and long passages. Today's schools still teach the traditional basics, but an additional set of basics, much more sophisticated, has been added to help people learn how to survive and thrive in a more complex world.

## Planning a Course of Study

You can't graduate from David Thompson unless you write a senior thesis. Washington state colleges are

supposed to dig David Thompson graduates because
of our theses.

> Terry Davis, *Vision Quest* (New York:
> Bantam Books, 1981 [1979]), 149.

Louden Swain in Davis's novel has fun in high school, but he
remains centered on his personal and academic goals. Like
many young people, Louden thrives on the excitement of a
challenge. He wants to test and measure himself against others
and against himself. Louden finds a way to channel that desire
and energy in productive rather than destructive or negative
directions. He chose the challenge of taking his school's honors curriculum because he wants, he says, "to wind up my high
school having done everything there was to do."

When students enter high school as freshmen—or when
they transfer schools—they're given guidelines for completing
that school's requirements for graduation. Louden Swain went
far beyond the minimum requirements set by his school. General requirements tend to look alike, with some local differences, among high schools. That's because the minimum
standards are set both by accrediting agencies and by requirements of post–high school vocational training schools and colleges and universities for admission. They're intended to
empower graduates with the foundation of knowledge and
skills that make them well-rounded persons who can handle
both their careers and their personal lives.

While some high schools are trying new approaches to
integrating occupational and academic studies and to using
cooperative or collaborative learning, many still divide curricula through the tracking system. Under this system, students
either choose or are placed in one of three tracks or courses of
study: vocational, general, or college preparatory. While every
student must complete a certain number of semesters of, say,
English or mathematics, the content of the vocational English
class differs in several ways from the content in either the general or the college prep classes. Students in such schools need
to know what that means in terms of the options that may or
may not be open to them when they decide on a particular track.

Because the tracking system forces students at the start of
high school to choose a particular direction, they should decide

thoughtfully and independently the one most realistic for their capabilities as well as for their goals for the future. If Bob decides as a freshman to take the vocational track, and then at the end of his sophomore year has second thoughts, it may not be easy to change over to the general or the college preparatory track. The curriculum in each of the three tracks builds upon itself year by year. Crossing the tracks—that is, selecting courses from two or all three—can sometimes work out to the student's advantage, but advisors and peers might make such a choice difficult.

Although pressure from parents, from teachers and counselors, and especially from peers strongly influences a young person's overall plan of study for the high school years, it's important for each student to make a considered choice that is best for her or for him. A number of resources can help:

Printed materials from the school, such as pamphlets and brochures, the school newspaper and yearbook, newsletters, articles and photographs in the local newspaper

Guidance counselors and materials from guidance offices

Teachers

Parents and older siblings or other family members

Students in upper-level classes

Graduates of the school who are now in college or in a situation similar to what the entering freshman is interested in

Adults they admire

Fellow students with interests, values, and goals that are similar to those the entering student has or wants to have

School and public libraries and librarians

After reading, discussing, listening, and thinking, the entering student might make a self-assessment on paper, listing strengths, weaknesses, values, interests, and goals. A student can also imagine what she or he will be like in five years and ten years (as Sylvia did in the introduction to this chapter) to help define what suits her or his interests best. That direction then dictates the plan for the four years of study.

While most schools tell students which track to follow, based on their past performances, test scores, and grade point averages, they also give students—when students ask—other options. Some students know at a very young age the career and the lifestyle they want as adults. But the majority have no clear idea of a career choice as entering high school freshmen (or even as college students). As educator/writer Charles Weingartner wrote, "Change is the central fact of the world we live in, and it is literally impossible to overstate the significance of this fact" (62). Earlier generations of young people tended to follow, in apprentice fashion, their father's or a relative's or neighbor's trade and way of life, for profession strongly determines lifestyle. But there are no such job guarantees today. Most adults will change jobs a minimum of three times during their working years, and sometimes that change will be a radical one. Many are and will be out of work temporarily or for an extended time. Meanwhile, young people's interests and abilities also undergo changes. So it's important to plan a course of study that accommodates this central fact of change to ease inevitable adjustment and transition as well as to keep options open.

Preparing a tentative plan on paper is the best approach. A school may supply such a planning sheet or students can make their own. Once an outline is sketched, it's easy to add or make changes or substitutions. The first priority is to make certain the minimum number of credit hours as well as the number of semesters listed for required subjects are met. After that, the remaining spaces may be filled in with electives and activities that help students develop individual interests in greater depth or breadth or that introduce them to something they haven't tried before. (See sample chart on p. 44.)

Schools vary in what they require, and different tracks vary in their requirements. For example, a college preparatory track may recommend a minimum of four years in a single foreign language and four years of mathematics. When students enter the senior year of high school, it's important to tabulate carefully whether they have the correct number and kinds of classes as well as the total credit hours to meet minimum graduation requirements.

| Credits Required | Subject | Grade 9 | 10 | 11 | 12 |
|---|---|---|---|---|---|
| 4 years | English | — | — | — | — |
| 3 years | History | — | — | — | — |
| 2 years | Math | — | — | — | — |
| 2 years | Science | — | — | — | — |
| 2 years | Physical Education | — | — | — | — |
| 1 year | Computer Literacy | — | — | — | — |
| 2 semesters | Fine Arts | — | — | — | — |
| 2 semesters | Practical Arts | — | — | — | — |
| | Foreign Language | — | — | — | — |
| | Other | — | — | — | — |

Total semester hours for graduation: _____

Some students are tempted to get all their most difficult courses out of the way before the final year of high school. It sounds like a good idea to have an easy schedule during the senior year so they can enjoy that year. There's a price to pay for such a plan, though. First, students who follow this plan get overburdened with difficult classes before they have the background and maturity to deal with them. But perhaps the highest cost is that without a rigorous senior year they may fall into lazy ways and lose the sharp edge they developed for learning, budgeting time, and practicing self-discipline. When they take the next step in life—be that further training or education or a full-time job—they're not prepared for its demands.

When planning a schedule it works best to vary the subject matter for a balance in complexity of material and in the kinds of homework involved. For example, if students were to make a schedule that required large amounts of reading in every subject, they couldn't keep up with it. Nor would they develop other types of learning skills as they went along.

When making a schedule for each new year of school, another way to get balance is to try to alternate subjects that are likely to be lecture classes with ones that require physical movement, problem solving, or discussion. The change of pace helps maintain mental alertness. Another way to get balance is to schedule a subject that's likely to be easier in between two that are more difficult.

In filling in credits for electives, students who are in the college preparatory track may want to learn a practical skill—for example, bookkeeping, appliance repair, or construction. Becoming proficient in practical skills can give students ways to earn money to help pay for post–high school education or to use as a hobby. Typing and computer literacy are important skills for everyone to have—especially in this age of the computer. More than one person has missed a job opportunity because they couldn't type.

Some other useful classes and supplemental activities that can be used in many aspects of life include speech and/or debate, journalism, leadership classes or clubs, and study/test-taking skills.

## Finding Good Teachers

"He has been a good teacher?"
"Yes."
"He is a good person."
> Chaim Potok, *My Name Is Asher Lev*
> (New York: A Fawcett Crest Book,
> 1972), 270.

Teachers earn reputations for being interesting or boring, demanding or soft, dictatorial or democratic, rigid or flexible. Word of those reputations spreads as fast as fire in a drought. In general, truth is at the center of these judgments, but the truth can be exaggerated or distorted. Another factor to consider is that the personality, style, and method of teaching of a particular teacher suits one student's personality and learning style but is wrong for another. One person's definition of a "hard" teacher means the teacher requires reams of paper work, quantities of reading, and the regurgitation of minute, not necessarily meaningful, facts for class recitations and tests. This same teacher maintains silence, conformity, and order in the classroom. Another person might define a "hard" teacher as one that demands and expects both herself and her students to think and perform to the best of their abilities and, through exercise and discipline, to expand their capabilities. This teacher holds lively discussions or groups the desks for different activities to go on at the same time. The involved buzz of learning may look like disorder to an onlooker, but such teaching/learning requires careful planning and management.

While different teachers' personalities and styles of teaching are suited to different types of students and their learning styles, the teacher is the central figure in a student's learning. Teachers who are good people themselves, as the one described in Potok's novel, serve the vital role of being good role models for young people. Teachers who are good people and who are excited about teaching and about learning can motivate even reluctant students. Their vibrancy is contagious. Good teachers have a command of their subject matter that allows flexibility of the methods they use to get the material across to students or help them to discover things on their own. Good teachers put their students' best interests before the subject matter. They encourage those young people who lack confidence in their abilities. They don't stand in the way of those who are pushing beyond the boundaries of where the majority of the class may be. Good teachers recognize, help develop, and bring out the special talents and interests of each person in the class to make the class richer for everyone. These teachers are learning as much as or more than their students as they explore the subject matter. Effective learning is hard work, but good teachers make the work worthwhile.

To find the best teachers, students can get advice from guidance counselors, other teachers they respect, students whose goals and learning styles are similar to their own, or go directly to the teachers who are assigned to the subject they want to take. Seeing the teacher in the classroom (even when no one else is there) and visiting informally makes an immediate impression and gives a feeling of how well that teacher's personality matches a particular student's needs.

Students don't always have a choice of teachers, but when they do, time and effort spent in getting the ones right for them pay big dividends both during the class and later.

# Finding Good Classes

The stronger the emphasis on academic courses, the more advanced the subject matter, and the more rigorous the textbooks, the more high school students learn.

U.S. Department of Education,
*What Works* (Washington, DC, 1986), 59.

This statement based on a study made by the Department of Education suggests that students do better when they set their sights on challenging materials. The caution here is that people need to be aware of whether they have the necessary background of knowledge and skills along with the capability to take classes with advanced subject matter. To grow intellectually, students need to stretch, but the stretch must fit each person's reach.

Judged strictly by subject matter, certain courses are more challenging, rigorous, stimulating, demanding. One student said, "I chose the hardest classes because they're the ones that are going to help me most when I go on to college." Another student said he picked the most challenging classes because that way he didn't get bored or lazy. A third student took the honors classes because she needed them in order to be admitted to a highly selective university. Still another said tough classes and tough teachers sharpened his intellect, and he enjoyed the sharpening process.

Honors classes generally demand of the students higher thinking skills and the ability to see relationships, as well as stronger self-discipline, self-responsibility, and self-motivation. They cover more ground and require more reading and writing and problem-solving than do most classes in a general studies track. Many high schools offer advanced placement courses in history, English, science, and math. Students who take these classes are given the option of taking a standardized test at the end of the course, knowing that if they score high enough they may earn college credit hours that will count toward a bachelor's degree if they enroll in a college or university after high school. Testing out of required hours of college work can save time and money for students as well as allow them either to move into a higher level of subject matter or use the extra hours for electives. Sometimes, though, students who decide to skip the basic level college course and move directly to a more advanced class in the same subject as first-year college students can be overwhelmed by a demanding content at the same time they're making a great many other adjustments to college life. Each student has to decide this issue on the basis of what best suits his or her needs and personality.

Vocational classes can be rigorous and demanding in different ways from academic classes. Students usually need to understand and learn how to use the vocabulary, tools, and procedures involved in specific businesses, trades, and industries. Vocational courses usually demand a broad knowledge and understanding of the particular vocation as well as of its tools and the skill to apply the information and skills in practical ways to solve problems. Vocational students generally have a strong aptitude for and interest in a particular occupation. But any class can be both academic and occupational when it's well taught. A current movement toward such a merging is growing.

Another kind of option in selecting classes is the choice between classes that are homogeneous or heterogeneous in the students who are enrolled. For example, a course in social problems may be open to sophomores, juniors, and seniors from all tracks. The primary motivation to enroll is that of interest rather than of ability or age. A class in social problems could be made much richer, in the hands of a good teacher as guide, because of the mixed backgrounds, experiences, and abilities of the students than if, for example, the class were composed only of sophomores in the general studies track. On the other hand, a homogeneous class is probably better in an advanced math course because each student is challenged both by the material and by the strong abilities of the others in the class. The pace can be faster than that in a heterogeneous class where some students may need to proceed at a slower rate.

Some schools can offer students the opportunity of combining work with a specialized area of study. For example, business students study in classes at school during the morning but during the afternoon hours are assigned to jobs that allow them to use their classroom studies in work apprenticeships.

Another choice could be to enroll in a college course, either during the regular school day or evening or on Saturday, at a nearby community college. Such options give students the opportunity to explore a particular interest in greater depth and learn if it is a viable area of study for them—and get college credit.

## Considering Extracurricular Activities

There it is: balance again. The most important quality a wrestler has. More important than strength, speed, smarts—even more important than endurance.
Terry Davis, *Vision Quest* (New York: Bantam, 1981 [1979]), 132.

This comment about the importance of balance in the sport of wrestling can be applied to school in general. Balancing academic classes and learning with an appropriate menu of extracurricular activities not only helps young people become well rounded, more interested and more interesting, but such activities can also help students learn and grow in ways the classroom setting can't provide. They can complement or enrich special strengths in individuals and they can give those who choose to do so the opportunity to explore new interests.

Some activities function in tandem with particular subjects. For example, Future Business Leaders of America (FBLA) gives business students an organization where they meet students from other schools in their district, state, and across the nation; share information and ideas; compete and cooperate; and learn leadership skills that carry over into other parts of their lives. Such an organization can help young people build self-confidence, self-esteem, and an awareness of a larger world.

Sports, both team and individual, intramural and inter-school, is another option that appeals to many students. Activities related to sports, such as being team manager or a cheerleader or publicist, can fulfill other qualities some students have who are interested in sports but don't, for one or more reasons, participate as competitors.

Student government can give young men and women experiences and opportunities in leadership, in learning how the political process works, and in working for positive change within the school. Like FBLA and similar organizations, student government participants meet students from other schools, go to conferences and meetings, and learn to make decisions for the good of a group.

Fine arts activities are another "extra" most schools provide. Students who enjoy, want a career in, or simply want to try out drama, singing or instrumental groups, art or photography will add knowledge, experience, and a chance to be with others who share a common interest.

Often other types of clubs are available, too, such as a chess club or an international or human relations group. Such clubs tend to have smaller membership and can build close social relationships among their members.

In the Department of Education study *What Works*, researchers say that "High school students who complement their academic studies with extracurricular activities gain experience that contributes to their success in college" (61). They might have added the words—contributes to their success both now and in the future. Scott Thomson, executive director of the National Association of Secondary School Principals (NASSP) said that while it's important for students to develop their knowledge in math, writing, foreign languages, science, and computer literacy, the "nature of our future society demands the type of skills that are best taught through student activity programs" (11). Student activity programs are the best way for young people to learn to both lead and follow effectively, to communicate well, and to work cooperatively.

Sometimes high schoolers make the mistake of avoiding all extracurricular activities—and cheat themselves out of an important part of their education. Or students sign up for too many activities, still try to maintain a high grade point average, and participate in activities outside the school as well. This extreme, too, can damage students in a variety of ways, one of which is burnout. Trying to do too many things can mean it's difficult to do any of them well or to enjoy what they're doing. They try to do it all in high school, their enthusiasm fades, and they never get involved in activities again either in college or in later years as adults in the community. These people, too, are cheating both themselves and others.

Some guidelines for choosing activities wisely include:

Being selective in both the number and the kinds of activities

Looking for those activities that hold a personal appeal

Trying not to be influenced by others to sign up for activities that aren't suited to individual personality, interests, and time limitations

Choosing activities that have strong, positive leaders as well as group members who are good role models

Having the courage to drop an activity if things fail to develop in satisfying ways

Being daring and trying something different from anything ever done before to see what happens

## REFERENCES

Binswanger, Robert, quoted in Associated Press news release. "Secondary School Years Are a Time of Preparing." National Association of Secondary School Principals, Reston, VA. Reprinted in *The Fort Morgan Times*, 11 January 1988: 3.

Cheong, Lau Kam. "Educating the Adolescent for Technological Changes: Some Implications for Teaching for Preparation for Adulthood." Paper presented at 3rd Asian Workshop on Child and Adolescent Development, Malaya University, Kuala Lumpur, Malaysia, April 1984.

Daggett, Willard R. "Vocational Education for the 1990s." Address delivered to the 41st annual Vocational Educators' Leadership Conference, Colorado State University, Fort Collins, CO, 31 July 1989.

Davis, Terry. *Vision Quest*. New York: Bantam Books, 1981 [1979].

Erikson, Erik H. *Childhood and Society*. New York: W. W. Norton, 1950.

" 'Four C's' Envisioned in Future High Tech Schools." *Education Week* (1 June 1988): 9.

Kearns, David T., and Denis P. Doyle. "A Business Perspective on American Schooling." *Education Week* (20 April 1988): 32, 24.

Keppel, Francis, and Jonathan Messerli. "Horace Mann's Client." *A Nation of Learners.* Washington, DC: Department of Health, Education and Welfare, U.S. Government Printing Office, 1976. 132–134.

Kohl, Herbert. *Basic Skills: A Guide for Parents and Teachers on the Subjects Most Vital to Education.* New York: Bantam Books, 1984 [1982].

Potok, Chaim. *My Name Is Asher Lev.* New York: A Fawcett Crest Book, 1972.

Sylvia, age 18. Personal interview, April 1989.

Thomson, Scott. "Value of Co-Curricular Activities Told." National Association of Secondary School Principals, Reston, VA. Printed in *The Fort Morgan Times,* 18 April 1984: 11.

U.S. Department of Education. *What Works: Research about Teaching and Learning.* Washington, DC: U.S. Government Printing Office, 1986.

Weingartner, Charles. "Relevance and Spirit: The Student's Viewpoint." *High School 1980.* Ed. by Alvin C. Eurich et al. New York: Pitman Publishing Corporation, 1970.

# Resources

## Fiction

Davis, Terry. **Vision Quest.** New York: Bantam Books, 1979. 197p.

Tough and tender Louden Swain, a champion high school wrestler in a small town in the northwest, is determined to excel in everything despite the odds against him. He keeps himself alive to whatever possibilities life has to offer and is prepared to do his best to make the best of his opportunities. But he's not your usual "perfect student." That's what makes him so appealing.

Eckert, Allan W. **The Dreaming Tree.** Waltham, MA: Little, Brown & Co., 1968. 300p.

When World War II forces a long separation of his parents, Will Wagner is sent to a school for the youngsters of such marriages. Feeling lonely and abandoned in his new surroundings, Will finds solace when he retreats beneath a bent old tree at the edge of a lake on the school grounds.

Glenn, Mel. **Back to Class.** New York: Clarion, 1988. 95p.

This collection of poems written in free verse explores the exciting and frustrating world of teens, classes, and teachers. Topics are real enough to prompt spontaneous student response, stimulating them to write their own poems in free verse.

Hentoff, Nat. **The Day They Came to Arrest the Book.** New York: Delacorte, 1982. 169p.

When the American classic *Huckleberry Finn* is in danger of being removed from the school's library, a variety of people object to its removal for widely different reasons. Add to that the complications of a principal with a history of censoring books, the editor of the school newspaper who's determined to expose the school's principal, and the school librarians who believe in freedom of speech. The tension mounts as Hentoff shows his readers that there are no easy solutions to the problems of censorship.

Holland, Isabelle. **Cecily.** Hagerstown, MD: J. B. Lippincott Co., 1967. 181p.

This poignant, inspirational novel set in an English boarding school focuses on Cecily, an awkward misfit whose ineptitude puts off the very people who most want to help her.

Keyes, Daniel. **Flowers for Algernon.** New York: Bantam Books, 1972 [1959]. 216p.

The theme of exploiting a human being for scientific purposes to study the human intellect is dramatically presented in the story of Charlie, a young retarded man who wants to be smart like other people. After experimental surgery, done for "his own good," Charlie's intelligence changes to that of a genius. As a genius, Charlie discovers after his initial exultation that he's still different from other people, still misunderstood, and avoided by others. He's alone and lonely. The experiment eventually fails when Charlie returns to his original low level of intellect. Readers may find it interesting to compare this book with John Hersey's *The Child Buyer*. The book was also made into a motion picture entitled *Charlie*.

Knudson, R. R., and May Swenson, eds. **American Sports Poems.** Orchard/Franklin Watts, 1988. 226p.

Both literary and popular poets explore all aspects of popular and not-so-well-known team and individual sports as well as the athletes themselves in this collection of poems that appeals to readers of teen age and older.

Lipsyte, Robert. **The Contender.** New York: Harper, 1987 [1967]. 167p.

Although this book was published more than twenty years ago, its universal theme, fast action, and strong writing make it still appeal to readers of all ages. Alfred Brooks, a high school dropout who seems to be without hope of ever having a better life, lives with his aunt and her daughters in Harlem. After being betrayed by his best friend, Alfred decides to try another friend's suggestion and get into boxing. Overcoming the cycle of losing, Alfred develops a winning attitude and new approach to life.

Stuart, Jesse. **Mr. Gallion's School.** Hightstown, NJ: McGraw-Hill, 1967. 337p.

Mr. Gallion may be sick and growing old, but he won't let the doors of Kensington High School, enrollment 600, close. Walking into a school where vandalism, truancy, smoking, and gambling run rampant, Mr. Gallion shows courage as he enforces discipline at the school—despite resistance from the school board—until gradually the attitude of the students and community changes. People begin to recognize how exciting and important the education process can be.

# Nonfiction

A number of resource listings that cover searching for trade schools, colleges, and universities as well as ways to get financial aid and career choice guidance are found in the list following the last chapter in this book.

**Academic Preparation for College.** New York: The College Board, 1983. 46p, $20 per package of 20 copies, catalog number 239200. Mail to: Department M94, College Board Publications, Box 886, New York City, NY 10101-0886.

This pamphlet outlines the skills and knowledge students need to succeed in college. It also includes a statement on the need for computer competency and for specific achievement in the six basic academic subjects necessary for adequate college preparation: English, the arts, mathematics, science, social studies, and foreign language. Helpful to read before planning a high school schedule of classes and study.

**Advanced Placement Program Fact Sheet.** New York: The College Board, 1988. 4p, free, from the address above, catalog number 235558.

This pamphlet explains what the advanced placement program is, how it's administered, why it was established, when and where examinations are given, and what publications are available to explain the program in more detail. Includes a list of College Board regional offices with addresses and phone numbers.

Carnevale, Anthony P., and Leila J. Gainer. **The Learning Enterprise.** Available from U.S. Department of Labor, Employment and Training Administration, 1989. American Society for Training and Development, 1630 Duke Street, Box 1443, Alexandria, VA 22313. 54p. First copy free, $5 for each additional; paper.

A report on job-related training, this publication recommends new curricula for general and vocational-education students.

**Common Learning: A Carnegie Colloquium on General Education.** Washington, DC: The Carnegie Foundation for the Advancement of Teaching, 1981. 139p.

A collection of essays by experts in the field. Articles that treat the subject of the student's role in school include Ernest Boyer's "The Quest for Common Learning," Frederick Rudolph's "Heritage and Traditions," Fred Hechinger's "The High School-College Connection," and Arthur Levine's "Prospects for the Future."

DeBono, Edward. **Teaching Thinking.** New York and England: Penguin Books, 1982 [1976]. 260p.

Designed for teachers to use in the classroom, DeBono's book presents the concept that individuals can use the thinking process to look at a problem or issue from every point of view through a series of identified steps. DeBono has demonstrated his techniques of teaching people to think using both logic and perception to live audiences in a televised series.

**A Guide to the Advanced Placement Program for May, 1989.** New York: The College Board, 1988. 25p, free, available from the address given in the first listing in this section, catalog number 201147. (The brochure is updated annually.)

The brochure briefly discusses objectives, offerings, and operations of the advanced placement program for high school students. By requesting the Board's catalog, interested persons can look for other appropriate information and aids.

Kohl, Herbert. **Basic Skills.** New York: Bantam [Little, Brown], 1984 [1982]. 213p, appendix on testing, bibliography.

Kohl provides a practical, insightful guide for parents and educators on topics vital to education. After providing background on the nature of public education and public schools, he proposes a new list of basics designed to meet the demands of today's complex society on teens and adults. A chapter on the "three r's" emphasizes the relation between mastering skills and content. He suggests practical ways teachers and parents can teach the basics students will need to deal with the future. The appendix on testing provides surprising insights into how tests are written, how they're used, and how they can affect students.

Leatt, Desmond J. **Developing Student Leaders: Exemplary School Activity Programs.** Eugene, OR: Oregon School Study Council, 1988. 35p.

The author examines the functions and effectiveness of student councils and student leadership classes.

McCormick, Mona. **The New York Times Guide to Reference Materials,** rev. ed. New York: Signet, 1988. 320p.

The guide offers a complete and convenient listing to what reference materials are available and helps readers find what's appropriate to their needs.

Suarez-Orozco, Marcelo M. **Central American Refugees and U.S. High Schools: A Psychological Study of Motivation and Achievement.** Stanford, CA: Stanford University Press, 1989. 182p.

The study examines reasons for the success in schools of many immigrant children despite numerous obstacles.

# Nonprint Materials

### The Art of Active Listening

*Type:* Video or 3-part filmstrip
*Cost:* Purchase $175
*Title no.:* CC-746-VS
*Source:* Human Relations Media
Room CC
175 Tompkins Avenue
Pleasantville, NY 10570-9973

Winner of the Society for Technical Communication, Cindy Award, this production shows that most people listen at about a 25 percent level of efficiency, but that good listening skills can be learned to improve work, study, and social relationships. Specific exercises in listening included.

### Career Direction: High School as Tryout

*Type:* 3/4" or 1/2" video, color
*Source:* Guidance Associates
Communications Park Box 3000
Mount Kisco, NY 10549

The film demonstrates how the high school experience can be used by students to identify the careers to which they might be suited. The narrative stresses that work habits developed in high school can have an effect on later career choices.

### Dealing with Decisions

*Type:* Video or 3-part filmstrip
*Cost:* Purchase $175
*Title no.:* CC-723-VS
*Source:* Human Relations Media
Room CC
175 Tompkins Avenue
Pleasantville, NY 10570-9973

The program equips students with the important skill of
critical thinking and challenging the sources of information
around them. It stresses the role of decisions in determining
quality of life and explores reasons for anxiety, exposes
ineffective substitutes for decision making, highlights the
importance of defining the goal, and summarizes the
prerequisites for wise decision making.

**Decisions, Decisions**

| | |
|---|---|
| *Type:* | 16mm film, color |
| *Length:* | 18 min. |
| *Source:* | BARR Films |
| | 3490 East Foothill Boulevard |
| | Pasadena, CA 91107 |
| *Date:* | 1983 |

The film presents a five-step process that can enable a
person to make decisions more easily. It emphasizes
knowledge of self in order to know what is important
personally, consider alternatives, gather information,
consider consequences, and make a decision and act on it.

**Destination—Excellence**

| | |
|---|---|
| *Type:* | 16mm film, 3/4" or 1/2" video, color |
| *Length:* | 20 min. |
| *Source:* | Walt Disney Educational Media Co. |
| | 500 South Buena Vista Street |
| | Burbank, CA 91521 |

The film encourages striving for excellence, stresses setting
well-defined goals, and introduces professionals at the top of
their fields as models.

**Dropout**

| | |
|---|---|
| *Type:* | Video |
| *Length:* | 59 min. |
| *Cost:* | Purchase $139 |
| *Title no.:* | S 00018 |
| *Source:* | University of Illinois Film/Video Center |
| | 1325 South Oak Street |
| | Champaign, IL 61820 |

The video attempts to identify reasons for the epidemic (30 percent in 1985) dropout rate in the United States and to identify programs that have been successful in reducing the rate. It emphasizes the necessity of a diploma for an independent life. The use of interviews of founders of programs to help dropouts, of participants in the programs, and of typical dropouts gives a rounded view of this issue. Gabe Kaplan stars.

### Education

Type:       3/4" or 1/2" video, color
Length:     15 min.
Source:     Agency for Instructional Technology
            Box A
            Bloomington, IN 47402
Date:       1983

The film examines humanity's shared commitment to education. It shows that for the children of the Tarahumara Indians this means commuting to distant boarding schools and learning Spanish, while the Baoule children of West Africa learn French because it is the language used in schools. The Japanese experience a rigorous educational program designed to help them succeed in a global society. (From the Across the Cultures Series.)

### Everybody Rides the Carousel

Type:       Video
Length:     72 min.
Cost:       Purchase $39.95
Title no.:  S 00314
Source:     University of Illinois Film/Video Center
            1325 South Oak Street
            Champaign, IL 61820

The video uses animation to present Erik Erikson's theory of personality development. In illustrating and explaining Erikson's eight stages of life as a ride on the carousel of life, viewers recognize what tasks are involved in each stage that must be successfully completed in order to move comfortably into the next stage and to do well. This understanding is helpful to teenagers in seeing how the stages they've passed through influence the quality of their lives now and that the choices they make now affect the kinds of persons they are becoming. It helps them to see both the consequences of failing to make positive decisions and change and the rewards of choosing positive directions. It also helps them to understand why they and others behave as they do—and understanding shows them ways to get along with other people better.

### How Green Was My Valley

| | |
|---|---|
| *Type:* | 16mm film, b/w |
| *Length:* | 33 min. |
| *Cost:* | Rental $12.50 |
| *Title no.:* | 5-0302 |
| *Source:* | The Film Library |
| | Learning Resources Service |
| | Southern Illinois University |
| | Carbondale, IL 62901-6510 |
| *Date:* | 1952 |

Based on the novel by Richard Llewellyn, the film dramatizes a boy's struggle to get a formal education in the midst of the coal-mining areas of Wales during the nineteenth century.

### How To Prepare a Science Fair Project

| | |
|---|---|
| *Type:* | Video |
| *Length:* | 25 min. |
| *Cost:* | Purchase $145 |
| *Title no.:* | CC-5010-VS |
| *Source:* | Human Relations Media |
| | Room CC |
| | 175 Tompkins Avenue |
| | Pleasantville, NY 10570-9973 |

The valuable experience of being in a science fair requires organization, planning, creativity, and hours of work, but the results are well worth the effort. This program acquaints students with the steps and procedures of preparing a science fair project for school, district, or state competition.

### Huckleberry Finn and the American Experience

| | |
|---|---|
| *Type:* | 16mm film, color |

| | |
|---|---|
| *Length:* | 26 min. |
| *Cost:* | Rental $17.25 |
| *Title no.:* | 6-1034 |
| *Source:* | The Film Library |
| | Learning Resources Service |
| | Southern Illinois University |
| | Carbondale, IL 62901-6510 |
| *Date:* | 1965 |

Narrator Clifton Fadiman shows viewers how to see the story of Huck as a viable experience that bridges time. Focusing on the epic qualities, he illustrates how and why *Huckleberry Finn* fulfills the basic essential of all classic literature in its universality. (From the Humanities Series.)

### The Humanities: A Bridge to Ourselves

| | |
|---|---|
| *Type:* | 16mm film, color |
| *Length:* | 29 min. |
| *Cost:* | Rental $18.30 |
| *Title no.* | 6-1595 |
| *Source:* | The Film Library |
| | Learning Resources Service |
| | Southern Illinois University |
| | Carbondale, IL 62901-6510 |
| *Date:* | 1975 |

The film offers a brief cavalcade of human cultural history, then focuses on a group of students who ask the question: Does it all matter? Through dramatic readings, a pattern of themes emerges that ends the film with another question: Who—and what—am I? (From the Humanities Series.)

### Looking at Tomorrow

| | |
|---|---|
| *Type:* | 16mm film, optical sound, color |
| *Length:* | 15 min. |
| *Source:* | Walt Disney Educational Media Co. |
| | 500 South Buena Vista Street |
| | Burbank, CA 91521 |
| *Date:* | 1983 |

The film introduces the concepts of critical thought and action and emphasizes the importance of critical thought to help people achieve the kind of future they want.

**Pearl S. Buck: The Woman, the Words,**
**and Two Good Earths**

| | |
|---|---|
| *Type:* | 16mm film, color |
| *Length:* | 24 min. |
| *Cost:* | Rental $17 |
| *Title no.:* | 6-1889 |
| *Source:* | The Film Library |
| | Learning Resources Service |
| | Southern Illinois University |
| | Carbondale, IL 62901-6510 |
| *Date:* | 1984 |

Hugh Downs shows a particular view of the world of the woman behind the writer, Nobel Prize winner, pianist, and philanthropist in addition to author. The example of this well-rounded person makes an important role model to emulate as well as introduces the writer of the frequently read classic *The Good Earth*.

**Reaching Your Potential**

| | |
|---|---|
| *Type:* | Video or 2-part filmstrip |
| *Cost:* | Purchase $145 (video), $129 (filmstrip) |
| *Source:* | Human Relations Media |
| | Room CC |
| | 175 Tompkins Avenue |
| | Pleasantville, NY 10570-9973 |

This program challenges students to question why many individuals, although gifted with intelligence, skills, and natural ability, still fall short of desired goals. It identifies the development of achievement skills as the crucial factor in reaching one's potential and examines the roles that cultural, family, and socioeconomic background play in determining the strength of a person's desire to succeed. Award winner: Society for Technical Communication.

**Roles and Goals in High School**

| | |
|---|---|
| *Type:* | 16mm film, 3/4″ or 1/2″ video |
| *Length:* | 29 min. |
| *Source:* | Films, Inc. |
| | 5547 North Ravenswood Avenue |
| | Chicago, IL 60640 |
| *Date:* | 1976 |

This film—primarily for teachers—presents child and young adult expert Dr. William Glasser extending his *Identity Society* and his *Schools Without Failure* concepts to the secondary school level. The film demonstrates how to handle discussion problems in the classroom.

**School Subjects = Careers**
*Type:* 5¼" or 3½" diskette, Apple or MS-DOS
*Cost:* Purchase $79
*Source:* Chronicle Guidance Publications, Inc.
Aurora Street
P.O. Box 1190
Moravia, NY 13118-1190

Intended for classroom use, the video helps students explore careers that are related to their favorite school subjects. A career profile workbook comes with the video. The toll-free order line number is (800) 622-7284.

**Setting Personal Priorities**
*Type:* Three-part classic filmstrip or filmstrip on video
*Cost:* Purchase $139
*Title No.:* CC-619-CS (filmstrip), CC-619-VS (½" VHS)
*Source:* Human Relations Media
Room CC
175 Tompkins Avenue
Pleasantville, NY 10570-9973

The program guides students through the steps necessary for making decisions about their goals in life. It emphasizes important decision-making skills, the need to clarify values, establish clear objectives, and develop strategies. Media & Methods "Best of the Year" award winner.

# Organizations for Students

Students who are interested in vocational or other types of organizations should ask teachers and counselors in their high school about ones available locally. Listed here are some national groups, many of which have chapters or might start ones where requested at local levels. For other groups that might be of interest, public libraries carry in the reference section the *Encyclopedia of Associations* and/or the *Directory of Organizations,* where information about hundreds of groups in a variety of categories can be located easily.

## American Academy of Achievement (Youth) (AAA)

P.O. Box 548
Malibu, CA 90265
(213) 457-8052
*Executive Director: Wayne Reynolds*

The purpose of this group is to inspire American youth to set high standards for themselves and to excel in their endeavors. It provides a forum for the discussion of career issues among students and adults who have achieved success in business, entertainment, literature, the military, the professions, public service, sports, and the sciences. It annually sponsors a Salute to Excellence weekend honoring 50 men and women of accomplishment and 350 of the nation's top high school senior honor students who receive Golden Eagle or Golden Scroll Awards. Annual convention/ meeting.

## American Industrial Arts Student Association (AIASA)

1908 Association Drive
Reston, VA 22091
(703) 860-9000
*Executive Director: Kaye Schaeffer*

Local groups are composed of elementary, junior high, and senior high school students presently enrolled in or who have completed industrial arts or technology education courses. The group's purpose is to help students make informed occupational choices through experiences in shops and laboratories and to help them prepare for entry into advanced trade and industrial/technical education programs. Provides opportunities for students to meet and work with leaders from industry for career information and to adapt learning experiences from other instructional areas. High standards of craftsmanship, leadership, scholarship, and safety are promoted, as are the development of consumer knowledge and appreciation for vocational skills. Leadership training is an opportunity at local, state, and national levels and projects and competitions are also sponsored.

PUBLICATIONS: *Advisor Update,* 10/year; *School Scene,* quarterly; also publishes *Chapter Handbook, Member Guide, Standards, Handbook,* brochures, and fliers. Annual conference, with exhibits.

### Distributive Education Clubs of America (DECA)
1908 Association Drive
Reston, VA 22091
(703) 860-5000
*Executive Director: Frederick L. Williford*

Encouraging leadership skills and vocational excellence are DECA clubs in many high schools and junior colleges throughout the United States. The focus for this vocational group is on the field of marketing and distribution (retailing and wholesaling) as an occupation.

PUBLICATIONS: *New Dimensions,* bimonthly; *Newsletter,* bimonthly during school year; and *Guide,* annual. Annual Career Development Conference.

### Future Business Leaders of America-Phi Beta Lambda (FBLA-PBL)
P.O. Box 17417-Dulles
Washington, DC 20041
(703) 860-3334
*President: Edward D. Miller*

Local groups are active in three divisions: Future Business Leaders of America for high school students preparing for business and office careers; Phi Beta Lambda professional association for college men and women enrolled in business, office, or teacher education programs; and Alumni. The club sponsors a National Student Award program based on national competition.

PUBLICATIONS: *Tomorrow's Business Leader,* 4/year; also publishes Advisers Hotline and Handbook. Annual national leadership conference, with exhibits.

**Future Farmers of America (FFA)**
National FFA Center
Box 15160
5632 Mount Vernon Memorial Highway
Alexandria, VA 22309
(703) 360-3600
*Advisor: Larry D. Case*

Local chapters operate in many public high schools for students of agriculture/agribusiness. FFA was organized under the National Vocational Education Act to foster character development, agricultural leadership, and responsible citizenship, and to supplement training opportunities for students preparing for careers in farming and agribusiness. FFA works with youth specialists in about 38 countries. Star Farmer of America and Star Agribusinessman of America Awards of $2,000 each are presented annually to two outstanding students by the FFA Foundation. It maintains a Hall of Achievement and a 1,000-volume library on agricultural education.

PUBLICATIONS: *Update* (newsletter), monthly; *Between Issues* (newsletter), bimonthly; *National Future Farmer Magazine*, bimonthly; *National FFA Convention FFA Times* (newspaper), annual; *National FFA Convention Proceedings*, annual; also publishes instructional materials. Annual convention, with exhibits—always in Kansas City, MO, in November.


**Future Homemakers of America (FHA)**
1910 Association Drive
Reston, VA 22305
(703) 476-4900
*Executive Director: Louisa Liddell*

Local groups in the United States, Puerto Rico, and the Virgin Islands include students in home economics and related occupations courses in public and private schools through grade 12. The club and classes help youth to assume leadership roles in the areas of personal growth, family life, vocational preparation, and community involvement. Two types of chapters are FHA, which focuses on homemaking, family, and consumer education along with job and career exploration; and HERO (Home Economics Related Occupations), which stress job and career preparation with the recognition that workers also fill roles as homemakers and community leaders. Cosponsors with Youth for Understanding of eight-week summer scholarships to Japan for tenth and eleventh graders.

PUBLICATIONS: *State Advisers' Bulletin*, 10/year; *Teen Times* (journal), quarterly; *The Adviser* (newsletter), 3/year; *Publications Catalog*, annual; also provides *Skills for Life* (16 mm film), *Stand Out from the Crowd* (videocassette), *Guide to Student Fundraising*, *Handbook for Youth-Centered Leadership*, and other chapter and classroom materials. Annual national leadership conference, always in July.

### Health Occupations Students of America (HOSA)
4108 Amon Carter Blvd., Suite 202
Fort Worth, Texas 76155
(817) 354-5047
*Executive Director: Dr. Jim Koeninger*

Composed of secondary and postsecondary students enrolled in health occupations education programs and of health professionals and others interested in assisting and supporting its activities. HOSA's primary aim is to improve the quality of health care for all Americans by urging members to develop self-improvement skills. It operates as an integral component of health occupation vocational education programs in public high schools and postsecondary institutions; encourages members to develop an understanding of current health care issues, environmental concerns, and survival needs throughout the world; and conducts programs to help persons improve their occupational skills and develop valuable leadership qualities.

PUBLICATIONS: *HOSA Leaders; Update*, quarterly; *HOSA News Magazine*, quarterly; *HOSA Directory*, annual; also publishes handbook, brochures, and recruitment package, and lends a slide/tape presentation on the story of HOSA. Annual convention/meeting, with exhibits.

## National Honor Society (NHS)
1904 Association Drive
Reston, VA 22091
(703) 860-0200
*Executive Director: Scott D. Thomson*

Has local groups of secondary school students in grades 10, 11, and 12, who excel in scholarship, leadership, service, and character. Selection process varies among schools, but membership transfers with a student who moves to another school. Founded and directed by the National Association of Secondary School Principals.

PUBLICATIONS: Handbooks. Annual convention/meeting.

## Quill and Scroll Society (Journalism) (QSS)
School of Journalism
University of Iowa
Iowa City, IA 52242
(319) 353-4475
*Executive Secretary: Richard P. Johns*

Honor high school journalism students are recommended for membership by their schools. The society seeks to reward individual achievements and to encourage individual initiative in high school journalism, creative writing, and allied fields. It provides information to editors, staffs, and advisers on all phases of publication work. Sponsors National Writing/Photo Contest, Current Events Quiz, and news media critical service. Through its Foundation, the society promotes research, conducts surveys, and grants eight or more scholarships annually.

PUBLICATIONS: *Quill and Scroll* (magazine), bimonthly; *Yearbook*; also publishes stylebook, handbooks for newspaper advisers, faculty, and principals, and other materials. No convention or meeting.

Individual states sponsor a state High School Press Association that offers workshops, meetings, and competitions for students and advisers to raise the quality of student publications. Such associations also offer support, both legal and emotional, to one another.

# CHAPTER 3

# Focusing for Success

[At his old school Jeff had been led to believe he wasn't very bright. But at his new school he has a surprise. He receives all A's on his first report card. So when his father tells him that he does have ability, Jeff is confused and asks,]
"How come I never did well in school before?"
"What do you think? . . . It might be worth thinking about."

Cynthia Voigt, *A Solitary Blue*
(New York: Fawcett Juniper, 1983), 151.

Jeff's father, Horace Greene, hopes his son will see that the actions of other people made Jeff believe he couldn't do well in school. As a result Jeff expected to do poorly. His self-esteem was low.

## The Meanings of Success

Success in school requires two primary ingredients: desire and self-confidence. While ability certainly counts, ability alone doesn't guarantee success. Other qualities are crucial to learning successfully, qualities such as desire and perseverance. It also helps to remember that people are intelligent in individual ways, and have learning problems in individual ways as well.

The scene above from Cynthia Voigt's novel illustrates that, like Jeff, students who think they can't succeed, do indeed fail. They give up before they even begin. Sometimes they look hopelessly at a classmate who seems to succeed in everything, the classmate who has it all—top grades, popularity, medals and awards. If a special opportunity or honor comes along, that person is sure to get it. But as poet Emily Dickinson wrote, "Success is counted sweetest/by those who ne'r succeed." Her observation suggests that the process of succeeding is the part of success that really matters more than claiming the victory does.

But success doesn't just drop out of the sky and light by chance into this or that person's lap. While some do have more things going for them than others do, success has to be earned. The Latin root of the word *succeed* means "to go beneath or under, to follow after," a meaning which suggests that achieving a goal doesn't happen instantly. Instead, success comes in steps, each step completed successfully and building toward the next in a particular sequence. Mistakes and failure happen along the way. It's been said that learning occurs by making mistakes, and then figuring out how to do the job or activity a better way. A small child doesn't learn how to walk instantly, but fails again and again before moving from the crawling stage to taking those first steps alone. Each time she falls, the child gets up and tries again until her coordination is mature enough to make the leap from crawling to walking. While the public focuses on the successes of people like Thomas Edison or Florence Nightingale, most forget the many failures each successful person endured, learned from, and overcame.

There's no magic formula for getting along well in school. But it does take daily discipline. In a book on writing successfully, Donald Murray quotes Robert Cooke, science editor of *The Boston Globe:* "Success at this task merely requires being alert, keeping up with things, and learning the language so that you can understand, minimally, what's going on" (132). Cooke is saying that people can succeed when they define a direction or goal, and then focus on that goal. Another way of putting it is to use the familiar advice coaches give—"Keep your eye on the ball." Those who would succeed at the larger goal of earning a high school diploma also need to focus on each smaller goal that leads step by step to that moment when they step up to receive their diploma at the graduation ceremony.

Success is relative. For some, success means simply having stayed in school and completed the required amount of work to get a diploma. For others, success means to crown their years of effort by being the class valedictorian. Some people will measure their success by whether or not they believe their schooling equipped them to meet the next step in their lives with the skills and knowledge they need to succeed.

When tennis champion Steffi Graf beat Monica Seles in the French Open semifinals, Seles said, "It doesn't matter I lost. I'm proud of myself" (*The Denver Post*, 9 June 1989, 6E). Losing (or failing) doesn't necessarily mean that a person is less of a winner. For Seles the loss was a victory. Success means different things at different times to different people.

# The Student's Responsibilities

Regardless of how hard teachers, parents, school, and community work to help students succeed in school, ultimately students themselves are responsible for their own successes or failures. While certain factors can't be controlled—for example, an ineffective teacher or a course that turns out poorly, an unsupportive home environment, unmotivated classmates, a given set of capabilities and talents, a physical or mental handicap—there are elements people can control when they make the choice to do so.

Students can succeed in school when they

Show up for class on time every day.

Come to class rested, having had a nutritious breakfast and then lunch, and having scheduled exercise into their day at appropriate times.

Adopt a can-do attitude. That attitude comes from having a positive self-image, knowing that the foundation for learning is in place, and being adequately prepared for the assigned lesson.

Keep an open, inquiring mind. Passive students either swallow whatever the teacher or the textbook spoons in or they let it slide off. Active students are curious, interested, questioning—linking new information and skills to what they already know, trying to imagine how to apply it in new ways. They wonder how things work, how different people view a certain topic or idea and why, and use their imaginations to ask themselves, What if?

Are willing to stay with a problem until they solve it, follow through with a task until they finish it, practice a skill until they master it. They understand that learning can't be bought at a fast-food shop.

Listen actively and respond appropriately. That means focusing eyes, ears, and brain on class discussions, relating the content in substantive ways to the assignment and to the unit of study, reflecting on how the subject connects with past knowledge and experience and with the present, and then adding meaningful comments that will stimulate others.

Have both the courage to fail and the courage to succeed.

Learn to organize information into main concepts, supporting evidence, and related ideas.

Prioritize tasks in order to use time efficiently and productively.

Keep aware of how others are performing as benchmarks to aim for or to avoid.

Build and keep positive communication lines open with teachers, counselors, administrators, other students, friends, and family in order to clear up misunderstandings *when they occur.*

Maintain a healthy balance of classes and activities in school as well as during out-of-school hours (including time to be alone, time to socialize, time to work, and time for homework).

Take reponsibility for their own learning, keeping realistic expectations for their performances.

## Keeping Grades in Perspective

I just stared at the hole in the toe of my tennis shoe. I never could please him. . . . If I brought home B's, he wanted A's, and if I got A's he wanted to make sure they stayed A's.

S. E. Hinton, *The Outsiders* (New York: Dell Publishing, 1972 [1967]), 15.

Ponyboy in S. E. Hinton's popular novel (also a movie) is pressured by his older brother/guardian to get high marks in school. Many students feel the pressure to get good grades. Such pressure can come from a variety of sources besides family members. Students feel pressure from teachers. Counselors and administrators exert pressure by making promises or threats. Classmates put pressure on their fellow students either to excel or to do poorly, a situation which can cause stress for students. The media, universities, employers all pressure young people to get good grades. In general for students A's equal success, and success in school is measured by how many A's they get.

Sociologist Gai Ingham Berlage pointed out that the dramatic changes in style in parenting by Americans since the 1950s have tended to put "unnecessary strain on children to compete and achieve, and often places unrealistic expectations on them" (1983). Berlage elaborated on this observation by saying that adults compare children's behavior and ability to school standards and norms. When parents exert continuous pressure on their youngsters and when students are continually measured against others, young people feel stress. Such stress can lead young people to destructive behaviors, to seeking escape through a variety of methods, to early burnout, and to apathy. He might also have pointed out that too much pressure leads insecure students to cheat. So while it's important to set goals, the goals should be ones that are within the reach of the individual who sets them.

The problem is that when grades become the focus for school, the primary purpose of school—learning—gets out of focus or doesn't occur. Good grades don't guarantee that people are learning and improving their skills. Neither do grades necessarily prove that one person is a genius and the next one not so bright. Grades measure only those things that can be measured—and they don't always correctly or adequately measure even such quantifiable achievement. Another myth is that grades predict whether or not a person will succeed in the future. That, too, often turns out to be untrue. Grades fail to measure important aspects of learning and don't test certain styles of learning. The irony is that whereas many people do recognize the shortcomings and the dangers of the grading system, it continues to be the system most commonly used to determine what a person can or can't do next. Educator John Goodlad points out that "grades don't predict compassion, good work habits, vocational or social success, . . . [or] happiness" (*What Schools Are For*, 63). Yet grades continue to be used as the school's means of being accountable to the public for the quantity and quality of teaching and learning going on during the school years.

While the grading system is intended to be a standard measure of learning, standardization doesn't happen. For example, the same set of papers graded by six different teachers (or even graded by the same teacher at different times) may be scored with grades ranging from A to F on any specific paper. Students who have mastered memory learning may score an A in an objective test but fail an essay exam—and vice versa. One person with a score of 90 gets a B while the person across the aisle who scored 91 gets an A because that's where the letter grade cutoff occurred. As a result the first is labeled a B student while the second one is an A student. If the same test were taken the following day or week, the scores (and the labels with them) might be reversed. And in neither case does the letter grade necessarily prove that one student understands and will remember and be able to use what he or she has learned better than another. And some students quite simply are better test takers than others.

Teachers often structure assignments to yield a curve of distribution in grades—that is, they want only two or three students to get A's and F's while they plan for the majority of the grades to fall in the C–B range. Teachers can be subjective in their grading, even in objective tests, taking off or adding points arbitrarily for this or that. They are influenced by students' attitudes, appearance, personality, and their perceived effort. Different teachers use different criteria in measuring what they hope students have learned and in some cases according to the type of students in a particular class.

Students recognize, too, that if they get an A or a C on the first assignment or test in a class, the teacher tends to put them into that A or C box for the remainder of the term. The student who gets a C on the first exam may have to work extraordinarily hard to move that C to an A or even a B.

But grades do provide tangible evidence of performance in school, and colleges and universities as well as employers consider grades as one guide for acceptance. Performance in school can indicate how a person may perform in college or as a reliable employee. And the rewards of good grades can be an incentive to do well in school for those who might not otherwise be motivated to learn. The consequences that go along with getting poor grades serve the same purpose with some students (Haley, 41).

When they can keep grades in their proper perspective—that is, understanding the rewards and consequences of high or low grades and at the same time recognizing the limitations of the grading system—people can more easily focus on the larger and more vital task of learning and of developing intellectual and other talents and skills.

## Making Homework Work

I finished my speech. Not only was I surprised by a round of applause, but the question and answer session stretched on so long Ms. Milliren had to cut it short.

"Thank you, Emily." She beamed. "That was an excellent speech."

Dian Curtis Regan, *I've Got Your Number*
(New York: Avon Books, 1986), 87.

Emily in Regan's novel was both surprised and pleased when her classmates were so responsive to her prepared speech. Before her name was called she'd been so nervous her head spun and her "mouth felt like the Sahara Desert." But Emily had prepared for that success. She picked a topic she knew well, worked hard to organize the information in a logical and clear fashion, and used her imagination (and her courage) to take a fresh and interesting approach. In order to have the time to practice giving the speech, Emily passed up the offer for a date the night before. She also decided against a pizza break with her friends in favor of rehearsing her talk. She focused on her homework, deliberately ignoring distractions, though they were tempting. Emily's hard work and sacrifices paid off, not only in a successful speech and her classmates' and teacher's praise, but also in being able to give herself a pat on the back and in strengthening her self-confidence.

While students tend to view homework with distaste, it's important to the learning process because it can

Provide background and preparation for the next step in learning.

Give students a chance to practice on their own the skills they've just learned. More practice means more mastery of subject matter and skills.

Expand and enrich material covered during the limited class time.

Offer ways people can individualize the skills and knowledge learned in the classroom and from the textbook.

Provide the opportunity to review and to get an overview of the material and to identify points of strengths and weakness. Discovering weaknesses shows students where they need to get help, reread material or do extra practice, or look for connections to other studies and applications in their own lives.

When teachers assign homework, they sometimes allow time in class for students to get started. The teacher can answer questions as soon as they arise or clear up misunderstandings right away. Students need to take advantage of this time to avoid frustration later when they complete the assignment without the teacher's help.

Some guidelines to help students focus homework productively and efficiently include the following:

Begin by clearing the mind of extraneous thoughts.
Prepare it to tackle the homework as an opportunity to

make discoveries and absorb information in ways it will be remembered and used.

Maintain a small notebook for homework assignments. Directions should be concise, clear, complete, and accurate. Double check the assignment before leaving the classroom and make sure the instructions are clear.

Keep a large calendar or chart on a bulletin board above the desk or near the study table or area. Long-term assignments can be budgeted for study over a period of days or weeks. The chart can also be used to budget time to get an overview of all activities and find appropriate time slots for the most important ones.

Set up a time and a place for homework that is appropriate to the person's style of study. Some prefer absolute quiet; others are more comfortable with music in the background. But distractions need to be reduced as much as possible. The right size and height desk or table and chair are important, as is adequate lighting. The necessary tools for homework can be kept close at hand, such as a dictionary, thesaurus, maps, writing materials, and perhaps a typewriter or word processor. Setting a specific time helps establish the habit of studying. If an appropriate place at home is impossible or difficult to establish, it makes sense to use the public library or to arrange to study in someone else's home.

Prioritize the list of tasks. Do those that must be completed first; postpone those that can wait a day or two or that can be done during a study period at school; eliminate those that can be cut out. Setting priorities not only relieves pressure on a person who's feeling overwhelmed by too much homework or who wants to put more time and effort on certain subjects, but also ensures the most efficient use of time.

Alternate types of homework in order to keep the mind alert. For example, alternate a reading assignment with a problem-solving or worksheet assignment and a memory assignment. Another way to vary the schedule is to alternate a complex and an easy assignment. Some students like to begin with the hardest and work toward the easiest assignments, while others prefer to warm up first with an easy assignment, then tackle the more difficult ones.

Set time limits for each assignment to increase concentration. By promising herself a short break between assignments, a student has a reward to look forward to. Crossing each assignment off as it's completed gives an important sense of accomplishment—a psychological boost that can also energize a student to move on to the next task.

Stand and do stretching exercises at regular intervals to keep from getting stiff or sleepy. An occasional high-carbohydrate snack helps, too.

Try using the following study techniques:

1. Prepare the mind for tonight's assignment by reviewing yesterday's lesson and today's class notes. Writing a one-sentence summary of the day's topic helps focus on the thrust of the material. Without opening book or notebook, the student might try jotting down all the supporting details, subcategories, definitions, rules, or anything else pertinent to the material. Next he can open the book and notebook and check to see what's been left out or was incorrectly remembered. This method helps remedy confusion or incomplete learning before the next step is taken. It also alerts students to points that need to be strengthened.

2. Learn to recognize when the homework isn't progressing smoothly and ask for help, maybe from a family member, from a classmate who excels in that subject, another person who's familiar with the material, a school hotline, the teacher (if the teacher has encouraged after-school contact for help with homework), or other available sources. (See Chapter 5 on "Getting Help.")

3. Do certain kinds of assignments with a partner. For example, memory work, reviewing for a test, foreign

language conversations, or brainstorming for a research project or paper.

4. Prepare work to be handed in exactly to the teacher's specifications (some teachers are extremely picky on this point and may lower grades if the directions aren't followed precisely). The work should also be as neat and easy to read as possible. Such care shows the teacher that the student not only cares about the teacher but about the work and about him- or herself.

# Test Taking

There are many different kinds of tests. They also vary in the weight they carry in an overall grade for a course. And students react to the prospect of taking tests in different ways. One extreme is the student whose adrenaline flows at being challenged, and the other is the student whose mind and body freeze in fear. Probably the majority of students' attitudes fall somewhere in the middle of the two extremes. The point is that attitude plays an important role in how well or poorly a person will perform on any test, be it a short quiz or a semester exam.

Confidence is the test taker's best friend. And confidence comes with mastery of the material. According to writer Jon Franklin, "The most fundamental truth about the cosmos is that big things are composed of little ones . . . he who would understand universes or temples, must first grasp the nature of their component parts" (91–92). The semester exam, standardized achievement test, or college entrance exam can be compared to Franklin's universe or temple. Those who have gone to class each day, listened with awareness, prepared each lesson and understood it, reviewed and questioned and thought about the material as they went along can go into any test with confidence.

Taking a test is an opportunity to take a larger view and gain greater insight into the course material. It's also an opportunity for the student to see how well he's mastered the course content.

Schoolwork, like caring for an automobile or a building or a garden, takes regular maintenance. If no one looks under the hood of a car until it breaks down, the repair bill will be costly. If no one cultivates, weeds, waters, thins, prunes, and harvests a garden systematically, the garden either withers and dies or grows into a chaotic mess where no one can distinguish the weeds from the flowers or vegetables. So, too, with school-work—if it isn't maintained on a regular, daily basis, an intensive crash study session won't repair the damage. While some students can retain the information they need to pass a test by cramming for it the night before, they will have difficulty remembering it the next week. They'll also have difficulty understanding how the knowledge relates to anything or how to use it. They do not master the course content. Even more damaging, they're establishing poor work habits and poor habits of daily living. Meanwhile, their intellects are not being exercised and stretched in healthy, meaningful ways.

To summarize, ways for students to focus for success on tests include certain strategies:

Adopt a positive, confident attitude.

Keep up with daily assignments and class discussions.

Clear up confusion and questions when they arise.

Focus the study strategy to the subject matter and to the type of test (objective, essay, mixture of the two, open book).

Budget time for study that is appropriate to the importance and length of the test. For semester exams, study can be distributed over a period of time, avoiding long blocks of study at any one time.

Find an appropriate study partner or partners, quiz one another, brainstorm questions that will probably be on the test, talk about, and then sketch out possible objective or essay questions and responses.

As with regular homework, take stretch and snack breaks at regular intervals.

Get adequate rest the week before and especially the night before the test.

Continue to review the material to be tested. Going back over points to remember while going to sleep or waking, or at odd moments in the day, such as waiting in the lunch line or going to and from school, helps fix those points in the mind and makes them easily retrievable.

Eat nutritious meals. They are vital for energy. If the test is long and a break is allowed, a high-carbohydrate snack can recharge body and brain for the second half of the test, just as walking and stretching will get the oxygen pumping through the system and to the brain cells.

Be on time or slightly ahead of time to put the mind at ease, and to achieve a sense of "being collected" and of calm. A hurried feeling can cause panic, and panic is not a positive mental state to be in during a test. Another advantage is that being on time allows a student—if a choice of seats is permitted—to choose a seat well located for hearing or seeing the directions and in a spot with appropriate lighting and away from possible distractions.

Clear the mind and focus on the test when the test is distributed. Look through the test quickly to check its format and instructions and to estimate how much time should be spent on each portion. It is also a good strategy for an individual to start with the portion of the test with which he feels most confident. Then the student should read directions carefully and make sure he understands them.

# Types of Tests

## OBJECTIVE TESTS

"Keep it simple" is a useful motto for objective tests. A person's natural inclination is to suspect a trick question, yet nine times out of ten the question is not a trick but a straightforward search for the best answer. In true-false questions words like "always" or "never" can mislead, but a careful reading tells the test taker to beware of such generalizations. Multiple-choice questions usually offer two alternatives that can be crossed out immediately, with the remaining two or three requiring more thought in comparing how the choice is constructed and how well it directly answers what's asked. Other types of objective questions include matching, short answer, and completion, in which blanks are to be filled in with words or phrases. Often key words in one question can help trigger the memory to call up answers for other questions. When a complete thought is called for in answer to a question, a correctly structured and punctuated short sentence should be written in. Any time the student gets stuck, he should mark the spot and move on, coming back to the marked place later.

When an objective test uses more than one method (such as true-false, matching, and completion), it's best to begin with the method with which the student feels most comfortable, and then move to the other types. In most instances, students don't have to follow the test in the order it is presented, but can skip around to suit individual styles.

## ESSAY TESTS

Some tests are entirely essay whereas others may incorporate essay questions with objective questions. In preparing to write a response to an essay question, it's useful to jot down quickly all the ideas and key words that come to mind that apply to the question. It's also important to be sure how the response is to be presented—using comparison/contrast, cause-effect, description, analysis, opinion, argumentation, or other writing strategy. Then the ideas can be organized into the most effective order of presentation. There may not be enough time for a student to write everything he would like, so it's important to check the clock at regular intervals, say, every 10 to 15 minutes, in order to be sure all the main points are included and the essay sounds complete—that is, it has a clear introduction, development, and conclusion. The same guidelines for structuring an effective composition should be applied in writing an essay question.

For essay exams or essay questions incorporated with objective testing, a good plan is to skip lines in writing the response. That way when the answer is reviewed, corrections or missing thoughts can be inserted on the blank line above where they belong.

Students who are experiencing the test jitters can find it helpful to take several deep breaths before beginning. Beginning with questions for which the answer comes readily restores confidence and triggers the mind to retrieve the information that is needed. Breathing soon returns to normal, thoughts flow with greater ease, and the test taking moves at a regular pace.

In estimating the amount of time that should be spent on each portion of the test, it's a good idea to allow five to ten minutes at the end of the period for going back over the test. Students can make sure directions have been followed and fill in any missing items. This provides time, too, to check for correct spelling, punctuation, grammar, and sentence structure. If a second look at a question seems to suggest a different answer, the original one should be erased carefully before writing in the new answer or if a pen has been used, the first answer should be crossed out neatly and the new one written clearly above it.

## COLLEGE ENTRANCE EXAMS

Just as a runner would never enter a race without an extended period of training and practice, so, too, a prospective college student should begin preparing—at least eight weeks in advance—before taking the required college entrance exam(s). Guidance counselors and/or school administrators keep high school juniors and seniors informed about test dates, signup times, deadlines for paying fees, and other related information. They also can provide sample tests, exercise books for reviewing the skills and knowledge to be tested, and the names of people or places that offer special test preparation sessions. Some schools offer the preparation classes during the school day or before the first class begins. Professional tutoring is another option available at varying costs, depending on whether the service is provided by an individual or private school, whether it's in an urban or rural area, and where in the United States it's located. The student will need to find out what the options are, and then choose which seems most suited to his or her particular circumstances.

Bookstores maintain large stocks of test preparation materials, too. Some students may choose to buy an appropriate review and practice book—or software package if they own a computer—and then set up their own study schedules either alone or with one or two friends who plan to test at the same time. Group study on this type of project has the advantage of the sharing of test strategies and of ways of gaining insights into the questions. The review also is richer because each person remembers things the others don't, so the pooled information benefits everyone.

Students should look at the test schedules for the coming year. Then they can compare the schedule with their own school activities and pick a time that isn't overcrowded. For example, Bob might see that an October date falls on the day after he plays in the most important football game of the year and that it's also close to the end of the first quarter of school when exams will be given. So he chooses the April date because it makes fewer school and activity demands on his time and energy.

April or June of the junior year is a wise time to take the test. Students have had the entire year to prepare. They can also take the test again later if they wish to try for a higher score. There will be ample time to take it the following autumn and still get college application materials in before deadlines.

Several hours' study each week, beginning about 8 to 10 weeks in advance of the test date, allows time to review the subjects to be tested and to practice test-taking strategies. The more practice tests the student takes, afterwards analyzing errors to see if there's a pattern, and then working to correct the weaknesses, the better prepared and more confident he'll be at test time.

Test strategies listed earlier apply to the college entrance exams as well. Generally, these exams are given on Saturday morning, most often at high school or college campuses. If the place is unfamiliar to the student, it's wise to visit the room and become familiar with the surroundings. Some students plan to take a large-faced watch to keep track of time more calmly and easily than by relying on the wall clock.

On test day students who have kept up with their schoolwork through the years and who have reviewed and practiced for this specific test can take the exam with confidence. Most of the test questions ask for basic information and require students to read thoughtfully both the questions and the choices of answers. People often make the mistake of thinking the test is harder than it really is. The students who focus on what is asked and adopt a can-do attitude have the strategies they need to achieve a successful test score.

## Getting Along with Teachers

[In the school he's just transferred to, Jeff] paid attention . . . during classes, did his homework without any trouble at all and made sure it was neat, answered questions when the teachers asked, answered exactly what he knew they were asking to find out if he knew.

Cynthia Voigt, *A Solitary Blue* (New York: Fawcett Juniper, 1983), 147.

In Cynthia Voigt's novel, Jeff Greene wants to take it slow, assess the situation, and get along with the students and teachers in his new school. So he stays in the background at first because he doesn't want to call undue attention to himself. In the classroom, he watches and listens to figure out what it is each teacher wants from the students.

Most students learn quickly how to please a teacher they have for the first time. They learn just as quickly the kinds of behavior that make that same teacher angry or frustrated. Because the majority of people choose winning approval over getting negative attention, they practice it—at least most of the time.

When students learn to get along with most or all of their teachers most of the time as Jeff does in *A Solitary Blue*, they can, in most cases, choose times that seem especially important to them to take a stand against something that goes on in the classroom. It does take forethought and effort; but by controlling their assertiveness, students have a good chance of retaining their teachers' approval of and respect for their behavior as well. Although expectations may vary among teachers, certain generalizations can be made about what most teachers hope their students will do:

1. Show up every day on time and in good health.
2. Act interested.
3. Be prepared for the lesson. It's impossible to lead a discussion with people who haven't read the lesson and thought about the material. Nor can the teacher introduce a new concept in geometry, for example, if some members of the class haven't mastered the previous one.
4. Listen attentively and respond appropriately.
5. Stay on the topic. Nothing irritates a teacher more than when a student asks right in the middle of a lively discussion, "What are we going to do tomorrow?"
6. Organize their materials and keep track of directions, assignments, tests, and projects; in short, take responsibility for themselves.
7. Try their best on any given day. Most teachers understand that a student's "best" may not be as good on a day when that student isn't feeling well or doesn't understand the material or has a personal problem as on a day when things are going well in that student's life.
8. Follow directions completely and accurately.
9. Turn in assigned papers that are neat and easy to read.
10. Volunteer, on occasion, for extra projects (but keep in mind that doing projects for extra credit to raise a poor grade may not clarify concepts that student failed to grasp).
11. Bring in ideas or materials that enrich the lesson.
12. Demonstrate by both words and actions that they respect themselves and others.
13. Indicate when they don't fully understand something, when they don't see how it fits in with the

rest of the material, or when they disagree with what's presented. Such comments are more effective when said respectfully.

14. Relate what is being learned in the class to other classes they're taking and to what's going on in school, in the outside world, or in their social and personal lives; be willing to share those connections with the rest of the class.

15. Expect the best of themselves, their classmates, and the teacher.

Not every class and every teacher will measure up to a student's expectations. But students can find ways to get along with their teachers and their classmates. When students learn how to get along, they find a more positive environment in which to learn. This is not to say that by "getting along" a student will never have problems. Occasionally a student and a teacher may have a personality clash or the student may be enrolled in a class that's either above or below his or her previous preparation and capability. Suggestions for what can be done in such situations are presented in Chapter 5 on "Getting Help."

## Barriers to Success

### PEER PRESSURE

I dropped out of school when I was 16. My grades were okay and I even liked school okay, but all my friends had already dropped out and I didn't look forward to going any more. It was too lonely there.

Christine, age 19, in a personal interview (May 1989).

When Christine gave in to peer pressure and quit school at the end of her sophomore year, her life changed drastically. She moved in with her boyfriend, got pregnant, and had a baby daughter. Then her boyfriend got into trouble with the law and was sent to jail. Christine and the baby were left to live with his parents. Bored, Christine began spending time painting, drawing, and reading.

When Christine was almost 19 years old, the director of the alternative high school called her. He told her about the school and said that if she applied now she could earn a diploma. But she couldn't wait any longer or she'd be past the age limit allowed for the school's students. Christine grabbed at the opportunity. "It was my only chance," she said later. "I couldn't pass it up."

For people like Christine, peer pressure can be a barrier to finishing school. At age 16 Christine didn't have the inner resources to stay in school when all her friends had left, so she dropped out. It takes a strong self-image and a clear focus on personal goals to go against peer pressure at any age, but especially during the teens.

Peer pressure can have positive or negative effects. Some students sign up—or don't sign up—for certain classes because their friends do—or don't—rather than because they're classes they really want to take. The same pattern holds true for joining clubs or signing up for activities or going out for sports. Peer pressure may persuade some students to slack off and get low marks because they don't want to be called "teacher's pet" or other derogatory names. They're doing what they think they must to win their friends' or classmates' approval. Others show off or misbehave for attention. And it's peer pressure that lures some of them to using alcohol or drugs, to driving dangerously, or to turning into "party animals." Some students skip school, don't do their homework, or fail to study for tests because of peer pressure.

While peer pressure often has positive effects, people should be wary of the kinds of peer pressure that result in destructive behaviors.

## PERSONAL AND SOCIAL PROBLEMS

Both personal and social problems can be barriers to success in school. While that list of possibilities could become overly long, it includes such situations as

A quarrel with a friend or a boyfriend or girlfriend

Being shunned by a circle of friends

Family conflicts or problems (financial, health, or a loss of some kind)

Frequent family moves from one neighborhood or community to another

Low self-esteem

Inability to adjust to new situations or to unexpected change

Inadequate sleep and rest, poor nutrition, not enough exercise and recreational activities, or not enough time for personal renewal

A schedule that's too full for one person's time and energy

Inability to organize well and to set priorities daily as well as for more extended periods of time

Poor communication skills

Failure to focus

The problems that can be barriers to success in school may grow to a level that makes it seem impossible to go on, or not worth going on—and that doing other things would be more interesting, fun, and rewarding. But students can overcome the barriers to a successful school experience. Chapter 5 offers some suggestions about what students can do about the kinds of feelings that may cause problems at school.

## REFERENCES

Berlage, Gai Ingham. "Middle-Class Childhood: Building a Competitive Advantage or Early Burn-out." Address presented to the 34th Pennsylvania Sociological Society meeting, Villanova, PA, 4–5 November 1983.

Christine. Personal interview, May 1989.

Franklin, Jon. "Mrs. Kelly's Monster." *Writing for Story*. New York: A Mentor Book, New American Library, 1986.

Goodlad, John. *What Schools Are For*. Bloomington, IN: Phi Delta Kappa Educational Foundation, 1979.

Haley, Beverly. *The Report Card Trap*. White Hall, VA: Betterway Publications, Inc., 1985.

Hinton, S. E. *The Outsiders*. New York: Dell Publishing, 1972 [1967].

Murray, Donald. *Writing for Your Readers*. Chester, CT: The Globe Pequot Press, 1983.

Regan, Dian Curtis. *I've Got Your Number*. New York: Avon Books, 1986.

Voigt, Cynthia. *A Solitary Blue*. New York: Fawcett Juniper, 1983.

# Resources

## Fiction

Bennett, Jay. **To Be a Killer.** New York: Scholastic, 1985. 154p.

High school senior Paul Moore sets aside his dream of becoming a neurosurgeon and thinks only of playing football. He neglects his studies, his grades drop, his chances of becoming accepted by a university are in jeopardy. In desperation Paul plans to cheat on his final exam in chemistry. Before it's too late, though, Paul finally learns to ask for help.

Crawford, Charles P. **Letter Perfect.** New York: E. P. Dutton, 1977. 167p.

Chad is a goof-off, along with his two best buddies. Their sarcastic English teacher shames them in front of their classmates, so they plan to get even. In the events that follow, Chad learns from the consequences of his actions.

Crutcher, Chris. **Running Loose.** New York: Greenwillow, 1983. 168p.

Appealing to both male and female readers, this novel is set in a small town in Idaho where a series of events shatters the happy existence of 17-year-old Louis Banks. Louis quits the football team in protest when a teammate, encouraged by his coach, injures an opposing black player. Louis's ethical stance finds little support except from his own family, and when his girlfriend dies in a car accident, his strength is tested to the limit. The story dramatizes how people learn more than what's in the textbook while they're in school.

Dygard, Thomas J. **Quarterback Walk-On.** New York: Morrow, 1982. 221p.

A young athlete's determination guides him to victory both on and off the field. Denny Westerbrook is keenly aware that he's no superstar. But when he's called upon to lead the team in the biggest game of the season, he proves that a sharp mind and a big heart are just as important as physical ability, in football as well as in life.

Greene, Betty. **Them That Glitter and Them That Don't.** New York: Alfred A. Knopf, 1983. 244p.

Burdened with irresponsible parents, Carol Ann Delaney—who wants to be a musician—has cared for her two younger siblings. Because she's half gypsy, her classmates and some of the adults at school haven't helped to make Carol Ann's life any easier. The music teacher is the one sympathetic adult in her life and creates hope for Carol Ann by giving her free music lessons.

Hall, Lynn. **The Giver.** New York: Charles S. Scribner's Sons, 1987. 119p.

Mary McNeal has the potential for becoming beautiful and successful but hasn't learned how to go beyond being ordinary. When her homeroom teacher helps her begin to blossom, Mary develops a strong attraction for him. In confronting the mutual attraction that grows between them, Mary learns to take a more mature look at how everyone needs to be loved and appreciated.

Hinton, S. E. **The Outsiders.** New York: Dell Publishing, 1972 [1967]. 156p.

This action-filled story of three orphaned teenage brothers, written by a teenager, continues to appeal to a cross section of teen readers. The novel deals with the emotionally charged issues of how social class, intelligence, dress, and behavior create friends and enemies both in and out of school. The two older brothers pin their hopes for school success on their bright younger brother, Ponyboy, and the pressure sometimes overwhelms the young teenager, who misses his parents' love and protection.

Klass, Sheila Solomon. **Page Four.** New York: Charles S. Scribner's Sons, 1986. 166p.

This story of bright, college-bound high school junior David Smith, Jr., tells how David's grades and performance in sports plummet when he gets depressed over his father's affair with his secretary. The novel explores David's painful search for his own identity.

Kroll, Steven. **Take It Easy!** New York: Four Winds, 1983. 138p.

Nick Warner has a terrific girlfriend. He is also smart, good-looking, athletic, and miserable. A junior at a private school in New York City, Nick is pushed by his executive father to excel at everything. In trying to please his dad, he ends up making his own life overly competitive. As a result, he loses friends. When Mr. Warner dies unexpectedly, Nick is alone, disoriented, and afraid. He begins to learn to think for himself and to finally take it easy.

Lipsyte, Robert. **Jock and Jill.** New York: Harper and Row, 1982. 153p.

Although Jumpin' Jack Ryder is an exceptional high school pitcher, the novel isn't primarily a sports story. A typical high school student, Jack shows his maturity by his interest in the plight of some extremely poor people he doesn't know. Jack's extracurricular activities lead him to discover some facts and values of life that serve to define his own character.

Major, Kevin. **Far from Shore.** New York: Delacorte Press, 1981. 215p.

Told in multiple first-person points of view, the novel develops a rounded image of 16-year-old Chris, who blames home and school conflicts for his failures and misbehaviors. But he finally takes responsibility for his own actions when he recognizes that he's the primary source of his own problems.

Pfeffer, Susan Beth. **A Matter of Principle.** New York: Delacorte Press, 1982. 181p.

When a group of well-liked and promising high school juniors disagree with their newspaper sponsor and print their own underground newspaper, they're expelled from school and bring suit. The story that unfolds doesn't glamorize students winning a legal battle but, rather, dramatizes the real cost involved in the process of defending rights. The main character, Becca, discovers a variety of lessons, including the fact that hurting people hurts.

Potok, Chaim. **In the Beginning.** New York: Alfred A. Knopf, 1975. 454p.

Set in the Bronx, New York, the novel concerns a gifted Jewish boy who becomes a Biblical scholar but who is plagued by chronic sinus illnesses. He's bullied by bigger boys, seems accident-prone—not to himself but to others— and feels safe only when he's within his own home. Yet David does emerge as a scholar and a person as he moves through these difficult years of maturing.

Rinaldi, Ann. **Term Paper.** New York: Bantam Books, 1980. 211p.

When her English teacher in the school she's just transferred to is in a serious auto accident, Nicki finds herself in the uncomfortable spot of having her brother Tony as the substitute teacher. Tony assigns the class a term paper, and Nicki uses the assignment as an avenue for writing out the conflict she's kept inside herself.

Voigt, Cynthia. **A Solitary Blue.** New York: Fawcett Juniper, 1983. 245p.

Young Jeff's achievement in school is mediocre at best during the years he's been told that that's all that can be expected from him. But as he matures and learns to understand and to communicate better with his father, he gets a new view of his intellectual ability. When he and his father move to another community, the transfer to a different setting and school gives Jeff the chance to test out his new self-image.

# Nonfiction

Bradshaw, Jim. **Homework: Helping Students Achieve.** 1985. 16p.

For information about this helpful pamphlet or to order it, contact the American Association of School Administrators, 1801 North Moore Street, Arlington, VA 22209, (703) 528-0700.

Ekstrom, Ruth B., Margaret E. Goertz, and Donald A. Rock. **Education and American Youth: The Impact of the High School Experience.** Philadelphia: Falmer Press, 1988. 147p.

A study of the factors that influence academic achievement is based on data from surveys of high school students by the U.S. Education Department's Center for Statistics.

Ferguson, Annabelle E., Ph.D., and Robert J. Shockley, Ed.D. **The Teenager and Homework.** New York: Richard Rosen Press, 1975. 157p., bibliography.

After explaining how homework promotes learning, the authors take a how-to approach to show students study techniques for various subject areas, including the use of reference materials; the roles family members play; ways students can judge the quality of their homework; and attitudes and planning.

Ginott, Dr. Haim G. **Teacher and Child.** New York: Avon, 1972. 245p. with selected bibliography and index.

The author's purpose is to help both teachers and parents deal with the problems young people encounter in learning by using positive reinforcement, encouraging self-reliance, defusing conflict, learning motivation techniques, and raising self-esteem. The avenue for this cooperative effort, Ginott contends, is that of open communication. He uses stories, anecdotes, sharply focused scenes, and sample dialogues to illustrate his practical suggestions.

Haley, Beverly. **The Report Card Trap.** White Hall, VA: Betterway Publications, 1985. 142p, resources.

The author contends that students don't have to be geniuses to get the most from their school years. The book shows parents, teachers, counselors, and students how to understand the learning process and the school system; and then to take advantage of the opportunities school offers, work around its limitations, and develop the student's potential. A chapter on study skills is especially useful for students, as is the section on breaking away after high school graduation.

Hodges, Pauline. **Improving Reading/Study Skills.** Dubuque, IA: Kendall/Hunt Publishing Co., 1979. 124p., bibliography.

Taking a workbook approach, Hodges includes suggested books for practice; readings and integrated activities; traditional and untraditional reading lists for the college-bound and college student. Practical, clearly directed study skills exercises help students review or acquire efficient study habits.

Langdon, Grace, Ph.D., and Irving W. Stout, Ed.D. **Homework.** New York: The John Day Co., 1969. 145p.

The authors discuss homework as being both useful and a means of extending and strengthening learning. Both the problems and the advantages that can come from homework are explored as well as ways teachers can make assignments meaningful and how students can turn homework into opportunity. How students' homework affects family living as well as how parents can help add another dimension to taking a positive view of an activity too often regarded as punishment rounds out the book's usefulness to a wide audience.

Mitchell, William, with Charles Paul Conn. **The Power of Positive Students.** New York: William Morrow, 1985. 191p.

The book promotes a program for increasing school effectiveness by teaching students positive self-esteem.

Steinitz, Victoria Anne, and Ellen Rachel Solomon. **Starting Out: Class and Community in the Lives of Working-Class Youth.** Philadelphia: Temple University Press, 1986. 273p.

A study of adolescents in three types of communities in Massachusetts and how they view the American Dream. Their attitudes toward school and work are an essential element of the discussion.

U.S. Department of Education. **What Works: Research about Teaching and Learning.** Washington, DC: U.S. Government Printing Office, 1986. 63p.

This pamphlet is divided into three sections and provides a simplified, quick reference for topics on research about teaching and learning: home, classroom, and school. An opening statement focuses on a topic for each page and is followed by lists of findings. Appropriate quotations about education enhance the research information, while source lists provide ideas for further reading. This and other pamphlets relating to school, homework, families, and teenagers are available from the Consumer Information Center, Pueblo, Colorado 81009. By requesting the Center's catalog, persons may select publications of interest that are free or inexpensive.

# Nonprint Materials

**Get to the Point**
*Type:* Audiocassette
*Length:* 60 min.
*Cost:* About $6 in retail bookstores
*Source:* Bantam Publishing
666 5th Avenue
New York, NY 10103

The audiocassette shows listeners how to learn to make their point confidently, memorably, and persuasively, focusing on how to "say what you mean and mean what you say." The presentation itself is almost as important as the ideas offered.

**The Secrets of Making Good Grades**
*Type:* 16mm film, 3/4" or 1/2" video, color
*Length:* 15 min.

*Source:*   Coronet Instructional Films
            Simon & Schuster
            108 Wilmot Road
            Deerfield, IL 60015
*Date:*     1983

The film tells the secrets six successful students have used to achieve good grades. It offers tips on lecture note taking, reviewing, reading texts, and test taking.

### Study Is Not a Dirty Word
*Type:*     3/4″ or 1/2″ video
*Length:*   10 min.
*Source:*   Seven Dimension Films of Australia
            18 Armstrong Street, Middle Park
            Victoria, Australia 3206

The video presents a guide to developing effective study techniques. Includes note taking and improving memory and motivation.

### Writing Skills
*Type:*     3/4″ or 1/2″ video
*Length:*   15 min.
*Source:*   Beacon Films
            P.O. Box 575
            1250 Washington Street
            Norwood, MA 02062
*Date:*     1986

The video deals with the six key stages of the writing process—prewriting, drafting, editing, proofreading, publishing, and presenting.

### Your Future Is Now
*Type:*     2″ video
*Length:*   60 min.
*Source:*   Great Plains Instructional TV Library
            University of Nebraska
            P.O. Box 80669
            Lincoln, NE 68501

The video covers the major subject matter areas and skills of high school education and their importance for future success.

## Other Sources

Many schools offer peer tutoring, supervised group study, or other types of personal study help. The school guidance office can tell students what school and community options are available for their use.

Public libraries, especially the reference librarians, offer a wealth of information and study helps to those who ask. School librarians, too, do all they can to help students locate needed information as well as provide study aids. Interlibrary loan services can bring resources not available locally to students, often within days or a week or two of the request.

A number of communities or regions direct homework hotline help. The telephone directory can provide that number as well as other kinds of educational resource telephone numbers and addresses. The school will also provide information about homework hotlines in the area.

# CHAPTER 4

# Learning and Growing Outside of School

[James asks his dad if he knows a particular song.] "Sure, son." Jerry Lee fiddled about until he found the right key. Then, looking straight at Grandma, he began to sing . . . James began to sing, too—a high harmony that perfectly suited Jerry Lee's gentle baritone . . . and they both turned and sang for Grandma.

Katherine Paterson, *Come Sing, Jimmy Jo* (New York: Avon Books, 1986 [1985]), 10.

The family in Katherine Paterson's novel makes a living as music entertainers. But music is also their happiest leisure time activity as the opening quotation illustrates. When they're making music, both their voices and their lives are in harmony. Young James, whose pet name is Jimmy Jo, was born with the music in him but has worked to develop that talent with the guidance of the experienced family members as well as through his own developing individuality.

But as the novel evolves, readers learn that the music the family performs for money creates competition, jealousies, and distrust among the individual family members. And as they draw Jimmy Jo into singing for money, his feelings of confusion and disillusionment grow along with his knowledge of adult motives and values as opposed to his childhood hopes and ideals. The source of his pleasure becomes the source of both his pain and his consolation. Jimmy Jo's education out-side of school teaches him lessons in reality and gives him an avenue for developing his unique musical gift.

---

What do young people do when they're not in school or doing homework? There are those who plant themselves in front of the television set, demanding entertainment. There are those who join the parade of cars and pickups cruising the local "strip." Others hang out at the mall.

But there are also those who take advantage of the time outside school to learn about life and enjoy it more fully. Many families rely on their teenagers for tasks like shopping, care of younger sisters and brothers, home and yard chores, and these young people make important contributions toward running their homes and easing the burden of working parents. Many teenagers are attracted to individual or team sports and get the needed balance between mental and physical exertion by play-ing on a team or competing individually. Others participate in clubs or church groups, gaining social skills along with devel-oping personal talents and interests. Or they have hobbies such as stamp or coin collecting, bird-watching, or photogra-phy, which can also form the basis for making new friends who share that special interest. And there are board games to chal-lenge and develop teenagers' powers to think logically, imagi-natively, and quickly. A great many high school students also do volunteer or paid work, learning about specific career fields and how to work with different age groups, applying what they've learned in school to on-the-job situations.

After-school hours also can be used for reading. Reading gives individuals the chance to travel to other places and times, meet people facing conflicts and challenges, discover different ways to view life and define personal beliefs and values. Such wide reading not only can be pleasurable, but also provide an important base for textbook and classroom learning. Equally important, readers can apply what they read to their own lives.

Activities outside of school give teenagers different ways to apply what they already know and can do. The activities help maintain and develop physical wellness, intellectual abilities, emotional and social well-being, and practice in managing time and, in some cases, money. Because outside time is limited, people have to make choices. Making choices gives practice in decision making.

Everyone has at some time or other complained that "there's nothing to do in this town!" Yet even the smallest and most isolated communities offer many possibilities. And the more people's own ingenuity is challenged, the more they get out of what they choose to do. For example, Danielle wants to take flying lessons but lives in a small town where lessons aren't offered. So she reads every book and magazine available at the library (both those on the shelves and through interlibrary loan) about flying and about the lives of pilots, real and fictional. She writes letters to pilot schools and to professional and amateur pilots and makes plans for the time when she finishes high school and moves to a place where she can take the long-postponed flying lessons. Meanwhile, she works on the physical fitness regimen prescribed for pilots, develops her intellectual skills with games especially designed for that purpose, and takes the subjects in school that will apply to her special interest.

## Unexpected Opportunities

Some activities outside of school, like Danielle's, are planned. But sometimes unexpected opportunities come along. For example, Jeremy's friend Russ invited him to spend six weeks of the summer vacation on his uncle's ranch in Wyoming. As a big-city native, Jeremy had always wondered what life on a ranch was like. The offer sounded like a dream come true. But going along meant he'd have to give up baseball this season, just when he'd worked up to play first-string shortstop. And he might be letting down the other guys on the team. After all, they'd all played together since they were ten years old. They knew how to play off each others' strengths and weaknesses. Besides that, his mom depended on him to get his younger sisters to their dancing and swimming lessons. Yet what if he passed up this opportunity? Would he ever get such a chance again? But six weeks was a long time. And Wyoming was a long way from home. What if he hated it there? What if he lost his spot on the baseball team for good? It was a tough decision and one that involved his whole family.

In the end, Jeremy decided to take the opportunity. Bill would fill in for him on the baseball team. Suzie, who lived just a few blocks away, agreed to take Jeremy's sisters to dance lessons along with her own sisters, and a neighbor would take them to the swimming lessons with her nephews.

Russ told him what to pack, and the two friends rode a series of Greyhound buses for three days and nights to Laramie, Wyoming (a learning experience in itself), where Russ's uncle's hired man met them in a battered red Ford pickup and drove them over a winding, bumpy road to the mountain ranch, and Jeremy had a summer he'd never forget. It was hard work to learn a whole new way of life, but exciting, too. As the summer progressed, Jeremy felt his body strengthen and toughen, his mind sharpen. He became an important part of a work team and was accepted into the ranch family. They had fun, too. Jeremy returned home with renewed energy and motivation for the new school year. He never regretted taking advantage of this unexpected opportunity. Jeremy's experience doesn't mean it's always right to say yes to all such opportunities. Each must be considered within its particular context.

# Physical Activities

Getting in shape strengthens the body, relaxes the mind and toughens the spirit. But it takes hard work and determination to become physically fit.
President's Council on Physical Fitness and Sports, *Get Fit* (Washington, DC: 1987), 5.

Whether people choose individual or team physical activities—or a combination of the two—physical activity of some kind is an important part of everyone's daily life. Exercising the body, getting the right amounts of sleep and rest, and eating the right food are vital to the ability of people to think and learn. That's why these activities need to be built into the daily routine and made an integral part of the hours outside of school. Physical activities demand adequate rest and good nutrition.

Dr. Ray Wunderlich wrote about the dangers of malnutrition in youth in *Kids, Brains and Learning*, saying, "In a healthy human . . . the matter of nutrition is [the] most important [element]. . . . It is now felt that the commonest cause of intellectual retardation, worldwide, is malnutrition." He observed that malnutrition in the United States is frequently difficult to detect. Nutrition should be monitored because, according to Wunderlich, the lack of nutritional foods "acts as a drag on learning, usually, and one has to learn in order to be intelligent. A great deal of brain injury affects the ability to read, write, or talk properly . . . [and] a child is especially crippled if he cannot employ language to the fullest" (20–21). Any classroom teacher can tell of apathetic students with no energy to think and learn or even talk about the reasons for their lack of interest. These students are the ones who don't eat properly and/or fail to get enough sleep and exercise. But a sensible diet on a regular basis seems the greatest determining characteristic in those students who approach their schoolwork with energy and motivation. People suffering from malnutrition lack the stamina and energy to participate in physical fun and activity, too.

Benjamin Fine notes in his useful and thorough family guidebook to education the importance of right eating habits in making it possible to concentrate in school and behave acceptably (306). Teachers at every grade level, from preschool through graduate classes, find it virtually impossible to motivate students when they don't eat right, get adequate amounts of sleep and rest, and exercise regularly. The *Dairy Council Digest* reported that 17 percent of the teenagers in the United States are considered to be at nutritional risk. During adolescence the body requires larger than usual amounts of iron and calcium in order to maintain strong tissue and enough red cells in the blood ("Adolescent Nutrition," 19).

Setting up a schedule to insure a healthy body and sticking to it pays off in many ways. Books, pamphlets, and magazines on this topic are abundant in libraries and bookstores everywhere. When people have good health, they feel good, and they feel good about themselves. And when they feel good about themselves, they gain confidence to learn and enjoy what they're doing.

Sports and other physical activities can be as varied as learning and playing games such as golf, tennis, soccer, and baseball to gardening, hiking, mountain climbing, fishing, rowing, biking, and walking. Choices allow individual, small-group, and team participation as well as scheduled and spontaneous events.

## Social Activities

I feel sorry for kids who don't get involved in groups like 4-H. They don't know they're missing whole new worlds.

Dawn, age 14, in a personal interview
(January 1987).

Not only did her activities in a well-directed 4-H club teach this young woman many practical skills and develop positive character traits, but they also trained her in leadership, communication, organization, and cooperation skills. Her varied experiences let her develop personal interests and friendships at home and extended her activities to include district, state, national, and even international levels. She was able to meet new people in new environments, travel, and compete with people she knew and with those she'd never before met. She found that often the people she enjoyed more were those who shared her same enthusiasms, whether at home or far from home. Her choice of friends, environment, experience, knowledge, skills, and options broadened as her definition of self came into sharper focus.

All communities—whether they're large, average, or small in size; urban, suburban, or rural—offer wide opportunities for social enjoyment and stimulation. The Chamber of Commerce, County Extension Office, city recreation department, public libraries and museums, and religious organizations can be rich sources of ideas for finding groups best suited to a particular person's interests. The telephone directory and word of mouth are also sources. If the club a person wants isn't available in a particular community, then that person might research the library about similar groups in other communities, consider finding out how to get one organized successfully, or start an informal or formal group around a special interest.

The values of organized groups vary, depending on the individual's needs or wishes, on how much that person gives to the group and wants to get out of belonging to it. Some clubs or organizations are limited by age, sex, or a maximum number allowed. Some are open by invitation only. To save awkwardness, hard feelings, conflict, or regret, it pays before joining a group to check carefully on points such as

The quality and style of leadership

Who the members are and what they want from the group

How the organization operates, both as a unit and for individuals

Cost, if any

Rules, regulations, restrictions

The organization's purpose, goals, and sample activities

Any options of roles and activities with the club

How much time and energy members give to it

What kinds of satisfaction members get from being part of the group

Club or organized activities build bonds of friendship among the members who share common interests, goals, and values. New opportunities for learning can open new choices.

Many communities offer classes in crafts, drama, dance, music groups, and sports. When groups learn and work together or divide into teams and compete on a friendly basis, individuals have many opportunities not only to test themselves but to learn about their own personalities, characters, values, and likes and dislikes. And they find ways to improve the parts of themselves they don't like so well.

Another opportunity is for older teens to teach younger children or to lead younger clubs such as Brownies, Cub Scouts, and 4-H. They might also coach younger baseball teams, teach swimming to children, or get involved in tutoring younger boys and girls in school subjects.

## Learning about the World of Work

I couldn't wait for the two afternoons a week I worked at the clinic . . . I loved the hustle and bustle. The staff handled everything so efficiently . . . [and] the doctors seemed pleased with my work.

Dian Curtis Regan, *I've Got Your Number*
(New York: Avon Books, 1986), 78.

Emily Crocker, the high school student in Dian Regan's novel, does volunteer work at the medical clinic where her father is a doctor. This brief quotation shows how Emily has entered both the world of work and the world of adults—and been accepted and appreciated there. She doesn't get a paycheck for her time, energy, work, and devotion. But what she does get improves her chances of making the transition to adulthood and of getting a desirable job then.

Because Emily works in an environment where people perform their work skillfully, professionally, and in a spirit of cooperation and teamwork, she develops a positive attitude toward work. Her strong role models both teach her and nurture her personal and technical skills. What she gains from her work at the clinic helps her focus her goals at school, forces her to make more efficient use of time, and gives her the self-confidence to make new friends, try other new experiences, and take some risks in fulfilling class assignments.

A 1983 study sponsored by the National Institute of Education showed that when high school students give service to their communities as Emily did in the novel, they

Gain a sense of responsibility and concern for the welfare of others

Develop the ability to work competently on collective tasks and to deal with adults

Learn to anticipate, or visualize, their own participation in adult groups and in politics

There are many opportunities to do volunteer work in most communities. In addition to hospitals, volunteers are needed in nursing homes, day-care centers, clubs for younger children like Brownies or Cub Scouts, church projects and activities, political campaigns and projects, service clubs and Chamber of Commerce activities. On an informal basis, young people can contribute to the well-being of others by helping neighbors or relatives with errands, yard or house work, letter writing, reading aloud to shut-ins, caring for younger children, or just stopping in for a few friendly greetings with those who are often alone.

Paid work can help young people develop the same qualities and experiences that Emily's volunteer work did. When someone has a strong interest in a particular career, looking for part-time work in that field can help him or her make the decision as to whether it's a career that truly is suited to that person's interests and abilities. It's also an opportunity to learn what must be done to get the position that's most appealing. For example, if Sam takes a Saturday job with the local veterinarian because he's interested in that career, the veterinarian can give Sam experiences that may help him decide if the career is right for him. It can also help him find a particular aspect of the profession that's most suitable and the steps he needs to take to become qualified as a professional.

But desirable jobs aren't always open to young people. And some take any job they can get because they want or need the money to support a car, buy brand-name clothes, and get expensive stereo equipment—or because they must. Some families need their teenagers to contribute to the family income because, for example, one or both parents are unemployed or do not earn an adequate income, because an illness in the family creates exorbitant medical bills, or during an emergency situation. There are those teens, too, who support themselves and live independently of their parents.

Jobs sometimes teach negative rather than positive things about adults and about work. In James Trivers's novel, *Hamburger Heaven*, for example, the main character, Kenny, takes a summer job at a hamburger joint the summer before his senior year of high school. It turns out to be a negative situation in every respect and eventually leads to Kenny's stealing money from the cash register. His very first day on the job foreshadows what's going to happen. Kenny dreaded, the novel says, working in this place, thinking to himself that he "wanted to earn his own money and be his own man, but he wasn't looking forward to slaving at a place like Benny Burger" (89). Kenny's work experiences move from bad to worse with each page.

*Washington Post* writer Dan Morgan described in the early 1980s the rapidly growing numbers of high school students who hold jobs in addition to going to school. Not only are more young people working, he wrote, but they're working longer hours and at different kinds of jobs than did most young adults of previous generations. The ripple effect from that has been that teachers have tended to lower their expectations of students because they lacked both the time and the energy to prepare their homework assignments adequately. Other negative effects are that students' attitudes toward school tend to change as do their relationships with family and friends, often from mixing with people at work who exert a negative rather than a positive influence.

Morgan's article pointed out that the fastest growing group of working teenagers is not among those who are poor but, rather, those who come from middle-class families and are female. These young people work to get money to spend, not to save for the future.

The writer went on to question what the priorities of Americans are when young adults spend more time working than they spend on schoolwork, when work draws adolescents farther and farther from their homes and families, and when these same individuals, feeling financially independent with a paycheck coming in, tend to disregard discipline from their parents before they're ready to be without that control. Supporting that observation is a Justice Department study that showed that year-round work and cars cause teenagers more run-ins with the police. Their problems are more serious than those of students who, although they drive, don't work both during school months and the summer. The study commented that a poor work environment implants negative feelings in teenagers about what it means to work, or about ethics when adult workers act dishonestly and unfairly in business dealings. The teenagers accept the situation as "the way the real world is" (Costelloe, 2 September 1982).

A 1986 study by Ellen Greenberger and Laurence D. Steinberg comparing 531 nonworking and working tenth and eleventh graders in Orange County, California, showed that among the negative effects on teens who work are that they become less involved in school, are absent more often, accept unethical business practices, and increase their use of alcohol and marijuana.

Young people can also get unrealistic ideas about money and about what wages they should earn. For example, young men working on oil rigs get more money than their high school teachers. That fact makes the young workers think it's foolish to stay in school. It also makes them believe it's their right to buy expensive automobiles and other material things.

A positive work experience, though, can develop interests and talents and provide an opportunity to learn from adults who are not teachers or family. It can teach the dignity of budgeting money and saving to buy something without having to ask for financial help. And the experience can help define identity and independence, and teach strategies for dealing with the outside world. The right kind of outside job can make schoolwork take on added meaning and show young people ways to use what they learn in school in practical ways.

The decision to work or not to work outside school hours or months is an important one that deserves considered thought. Some questions that can help make that decision include:

1. Is the money a necessity or a luxury?
2. How much time (and when) is required?
3. What must be given up in order to take the job?
4. How will the job help the employee learn more about what it means to work, about getting along with people, and about developing productive work skills and habits and positive attitudes?
5. Will working enhance or take away from schoolwork and activities?

6. What impact might the job have on family and friends?

7. If the job doesn't work out, what options are available?

# Focusing on Cultural Activities

Certain things are given, and it is for man to use them to bring goodness into the world. The Master of the Universe gives us glimpses, only glimpses. It is for us to open our eyes wide.

Chaim Potok, *My Name Is Asher Lev* (New York: A Fawcett Crest Book, 1972), 271.

In this quotation, a rabbi talks with the extraordinarily gifted young artist about his genius. The story of Asher Lev is the story of the pain and the ecstasy that are inherent in the life of a gifted person. The rabbi cautions Asher Lev to focus his talent to "bring goodness into the world." His advice suggests that any skill, knowledge, or talent may be used for constructive or for destructive purposes. The rabbi worries that conscience and a sense of moral values must accompany natural gifts to ensure that they will be used to make life better for others rather than for personal gain or for inhumane purposes.

The arts and humanities—those parts of a society regarded as its "culture"—create a balance between matters of the heart and spirit and matters of the mind and reason. Both are needed; neither should exclude the other. Archibald MacLeish, known primarily for his works of poetry and drama, wrote that "It is the work of art that creates the human perspective in which information turns to truth" (Goodman, 162). Because historically the arts have been considered a nice but unnecessary frill in the school curriculum, most people get much of this part of their education outside the school setting.

Learning and growing culturally is a vital aspect of what it means to be fully human. Although only a small percentage of people become professional in the arts (and an even smaller percentage of those, like a Mozart or a Van Gogh, are true geniuses), every person has the capacity to develop artistic talents in one or several forms. The impulse to decorate the cover of a notebook or to wear certain styles and colors of clothes is one everyone knows and shares. The expression of such decoration reveals individual personality as well as the human need for truth and beauty. Numerous articles and books have been published on the art of photography, conversation, cooking, living, loving, and so on. The art of anything suggests that its techniques have been mastered and then raised to another level that goes beyond mere mechanical performance—it can then be played upon to express the master's inner self and values. But people don't have to be masters of the arts to be able to use and develop enough talent of their own to make their lives richer, fuller, and more enjoyable.

Any community's parks, zoos, art galleries, theaters, performing arts centers, concert halls, gardens, and libraries are clearly places for cultural growth and nurture. Many people choose to take private or group lessons in singing, drama, art, dance, playing musical instruments, or writing. And many participate in community acting groups, art clubs, symphonies or bands or choruses, nature clubs, or book discussion groups. Often an interest or talent shared with others forms the basis for new friendships and new learning. Interests in the sciences and in math have their human side, too. Talents and interests developed outside of school can be applied to extracurricular school activities, making them more enjoyable because the person participating has gained greater mastery of their skills and knowledge.

Maybe the best, least expensive, and most flexible means to cultural growth is through wide reading, as mentioned earlier in this chapter. Readers learn about themselves and others and about why they respond to one another and to certain situations as they do. Readers of books can discover the answers to questions they've wondered about or to problems they've been unable to solve. Through vicarious experience, they can think about how they would behave in certain circumstances and role-play various options for the best effect. Books at once offer escape from daily pressures and stretch readers' minds and imaginations.

One author referred to books as being "windows" and "mirrors"—they let their readers look out at other worlds and people and at the same time see themselves in the mirror and reflect on the image.

The natural accompaniment to reading is writing. It's been observed that people learn letter writing better outside of school than in school. Letters to friends, to pen pals, to a variety of persons or institutions asking for information or help are usually written at home. Many people enjoy keeping personal journals or diaries. Such writing develops writing ability and offers opportunities for problem solving, decision making, and relating to and sharing with others. It is also fun to play with words and discover new ways of using language. Again this kind of practice and experience applies to what students do at school and at work later.

Learning and growing outside of school develops the whole person in ways that can make school more interesting and useful. It also builds a broad foundation on which to build the kind of formal learning that goes on in school. But for those who find it difficult to succeed in school, learning and succeeding outside of school may be even more important. Their successes outside of school tell them they are worthwhile; their successes help them strengthen and keep their self-esteem.

## REFERENCES

"Adolescent Nutrition: Issues and Challenges." *Dairy Council Digest* 58, no. 4 (July–August 1987): 19–23.

Costelloe, Kevin. "Cars, Jobs Cause Teen Trouble." Associated Press article. *The Denver Post*, 2 September 1982.

Dawn, age 14. Personal interview, January 1987.

Fine, Benjamin. *The Modern Family Guide to Education*. New York: Doubleday & Co., 1950.

Goodman, Leroy V. "A Special Telling of History." *A Nation of Learners*. Washington, DC: Department of Health, Education and Welfare, U.S. Government Printing Office, 1976. 162.

Greenberger, Ellen, and Laurence Steinberg. *When Teenagers Work*. New York: Basic Books, Inc., 1986.

Morgan, Dan. "Are Working Teenagers Shortchanging Themselves?" Copyright, *The Washington Post*. *The Sunday Denver Post*, 21 November 1982. 50, 58, 60.

Paterson, Katherine. *Come Sing, Jimmy Jo*. New York: Avon Books, 1986 [1985].

Potok, Chaim. *My Name Is Asher Lev*. New York: A Fawcett Crest Book, 1972.

President's Council on Physical Fitness and Sports. *Get Fit*. Washington, DC: 1987.

Regan, Dian Curtis. *I've Got Your Number*. New York: Avon Books, 1986.

Trivers, James. *Hamburger Heaven*. New York: Avon Books, 1976.

Wunderlich, Dr. Ray C. *Kids, Brains and Learning*. St. Petersburg, FL: Johnny Reads, Inc., 1970.

# Resources

## Fiction

Bacon, Katharine J. **Shadow and Light.** New York: McElderry/ Macmillan, 1987. 208p.

Emma spends the summer on her grandmother's farm in Vermont, working with horses and hoping to develop a report on horses to enter in a state-wide competition. The special closeness between Emma and her grandmother intensifies when Emma realizes that her grandmother is acting differently. This book was one of those chosen by young adults for the Iowa Books Poll.

Borland, Hal. **When the Legends Die.** Hagerstown, MD: J. B. Lippincott Co., 1963. 288p.

After his parents die, a young Indian boy, brought up in the ways of his people, is forced to conform to a culture vastly different from his own. He spends years of striving and pain trying to define his own identity in the world of rodeo. This classic story is also a movie.

Bradbury, Ray. **Dandelion Wine.** New York: Bantam Books, 1978 [1957]. 239p.

This novel is set in a small town in Illinois just before the Great Depression. A teenage boy spends a summer discovering his identity while staying in his grandparents' home. The story is an intriguing mixture of real-life people, fantasy, and mysticism. A classic.

Cohen, Barbara. **People Like Us.** New York: Bantam Books, 1987. 160p.

Dinah Adler runs into trouble with her family when she
wants to date Geoff, who is not of her family's religion and
ethnic group. To Dinah, her parents' attitude is hypocritical,
and she must decide whether to submit to their wishes or to
establish her own personal and religious identity.

Cormier, Robert. **8 Plus 1.** New York: Bantam Books, 1982.
172p.

This collection of short stories by the author of *The Chocolate
War* and *After the First Death* dramatizes a variety of personal
relationships, such as friend to friend, father to daughter,
young to old. Cormier's warmth, compassion, and special
character are revealed in the introductions he has written to
each story.

Gallo, Donald R., ed. **Sixteen Short Stories by Outstanding
Writers for Young Adults.** New York: Delacorte Press, 1984.
179p.

This collection of short stories by authors young people know
well—including Richard Peck, Robert Lipsyte, M. E. Kerr,
and Norma Fox Mazer—addresses teenage concerns at the
same time it gives them a wide variety of entertaining stories.
Each story is followed by a biographical sketch of the author.
Reader activities are suggested at the end of the book.

————.**Visions: Nineteen Short Stories by Outstanding
Authors for Young Adults.** New York: Delacorte Press, 1987.
229p.

The wide range of previously unpublished stories by authors
including Fran Arrick, Sue Ellen Bridgers, Walter Dean
Myers, Todd Strasser, and Jane Yolen appeals to all types of
readers. The stories are grouped in themes—Figments,
Adjustments, Conflicts, Choices, Illuminations, and
Kinships—and include tales of humor, romance, real-life
situations, fantasy, and science fiction. A biographical sketch
of the author follows each story.

Gold, Robert S. **Point of Departure.** New York: Dell
Publishing, 1967. 190p.

This collection of 19 previously published stories by well-known authors, such as Jesse Stuart, William Saroyan, Carson McCullers, John Updike, and Bernard Malamud, addresses the many aspects of youth and discovery.

Knudson, R. R. **Fox Running.** New York: Avon Books, 1975. 125p.

The story of two young women runners from very different worlds–one a burned-out Olympic gold medalist, Kathy "Sudden" Hart, the other a Mescalero Apache Indian, Fox Running—reveals their growing friendship and their need to discover all things again through each other's eyes. Readers will share the intense experience of competitive running along with the dual heroines as well relate to their unusual friendship.

Lasky, Kathryn. **Home Free.** New York: Dell Publishing, 1988. 245p.

Sam, age 15, helps a dying adult lure eagles to a place where they can survive when their natural habitat is flooded. Sam becomes friendly with an eagle he calls Lucy, and communicates with her, in a world half real, half fantasy. Sam learns from the eagles about what's important in life.

Laurie, Dick, et al., eds. **Smart Like Me.** Brooklyn, NY: Hanging Loose Press, 1989. 159p.

The collection of poems written by young writers over the past 20 years speaks in real voices to the teen reader. The poems were originally published in *Hanging Loose Magazine*, a national poetry journal that recognizes excellence in the work of high school poets. This source might also serve as an outlet for students' work.

Peyton, K. M. **Prove Yourself a Hero.** New York: Dell Publishing, 1980 [1977]. 191p.

Jonathan Meredith is kidnapped and held for ransom for three days. The experiences he has during those three days and the difficulties he encounters later with family, friends, and school make him take a new look at his own and others' lives. The story's suspense keeps the reader turning the pages; the unfolding of character allows insights into human nature.

Potok, Chaim, **Davita's Harp.** New York: A Fawcett Crest Book, 1985. 438p.

When her parents move frequently, Davita must adjust to each new school, set of teachers, and classmates. Her parents' political activities and meetings cause Davita to have some confusing and embarrassing confrontations at school and make her begin to reflect on her own values. A few weeks' vacation gives her the distance and time she needs to sort things out in her mind.

Regan, Dian Curtis. **I've Got Your Number.** New York: Avon Books, 1986. 138p.

Emily Crocker keeps her mind on doing well at school and developing new interests and friendships through her school and community activities. School, family, friends, and volunteer work help Emily mature and define her own identity.

Trivers, James. **Hamburger Heaven.** New York: Avon Books, 1976. 125p.

Kenny's first job in a local hamburger joint teaches him all the wrong things about work—the mindless routine, a dishonest boss who takes advantage of him, an unpleasant environment, and yielding to the temptation to help himself to the money that will buy the things he wants.

Walden, Amelia. **Heartbreak Tennis.** Philadelphia: Westminster Press, 1977. 168p.

When Rod Marshall, a tennis pro, offers to coach Cindy Banner during the summer break, she sees his offer as the chance of a lifetime to go somewhere with her tennis. Her discipline, hard work, and desire are the right combination to accompany her natural talent. As Cindy advances up the ladder of competition, she discovers there's more to playing this level of tennis than being a strong and smart athlete. She makes friends with Jennifer, a former Wimbledon champion, who helps coach Cindy—and also helps her examine her motives for competing. And a new romance leaves Cindy's former boyfriend Jimsy waiting on the sidelines. By the end of the story, Cindy's summer experience leaves her facing major decisions that will shape the direction of her future.

Waters, Frank. **The Man Who Killed the Deer.** New York: Pocket Books, 1974 [1941]. 217p.

This wonderfully written novel describes the inner and outer conflicts of a young Pueblo Indian as he's caught between his native culture and that of the white man. He fits into neither world. An older man in the tribe tells the young man to listen to his heart, his mind, his body, and not quarrel with them if he is to be at peace inside himself. Readers examine their own identities and values as they watch the young Indian struggle with his own.

Zindel, Paul. **Harry & Hortense at Hormone High.** New York: Bantam Books, 1985 [1984]. 150p.

Harry Hickey's and Hortense McCoy's lives change dramatically when a new student at school, Jason Rohr, who looks like a Greek god, confides in them that he believes he's the reincarnation of the demigod Icarus. The author uses Jason to address the question of where all the heroes have gone. As always, Zindel's playfulness with words uses humor to deliver a serious message.

————. **The Pigman.** New York: Dell Publishing, 1968. 159p.

At school, John puts on a clown act; Lorraine's too serious. Then outside of school John and an old man, Mr. Pignati, "the Pigman," who befriends the two teenagers, show Lorraine how to have fun. Both John and Lorraine have similar problems—they find it impossible to communicate with their respective parents; but they find they can talk freely with the Pigman.

Zolotow, Charlotte, ed. **Early Sorrow.** New York: Harper and Row, 1986. 212p.

This collection of stories by talented writers addresses the theme of traumatic moments in the lives of adolescents. For example, the condition of being "different," the experience of a mother's death, and the need to love one's parents even when they are worthless are among the settings for early sorrows.

# Nonfiction

**All About Letters,** rev. ed. U.S. Postal Service and National Council of Teachers of English, 1982. 64p. $2.50.

Many have said that the art of letter writing is dead. This useful booklet proclaims the joys of letter writing and also tells how to write various types of letters from the friendly letter to the letter of complaint or a letter of application. It also gives directions for typing addresses on envelopes, shows the differences between the previously accepted method for addressing and the new form, lists the two-letter abbreviations for each state, and gives the names and addresses of places from which students might want to request information of various types. To order the booklet, write Fulfillment Department, National Council of Teachers of English, 1111 Kenyon Road, Urbana, IL 61801.

Brondino, Jeanne, and the Parent/Teen Book Group. **Raising Each Other: A Book for Teens and Parents.** Claremont, CA: Hunter House, 1988. 147p.

Using essays and interviews with their parents, high school students reveal their feelings about relationships between adolescents and parents.

Council on Standards for International Educational Travel (CSIET). **Advisory List of International Educational Travel and Exchange Programs, 1988.** Reston, VA: CSIET, 1987. 104p.

This handy guide is packed with information and necessary details for those students interested in exchange programs of travel and education both abroad and nearer home. The information is compiled annually for the programs available during that school year and summer. A centerfold, "Programs at a Glance," is a good starting point that tells students which programs they want to look at more closely and which they can cross off the list without spending further time. The pamphlet is available at a nominal cost by writing either CSIET, 1906 Association Drive, Reston, VA 22091, (703) 860-5317 or Consumer Information Center, P.O. Box 100, Pueblo, CO 81002.

Cuthbertson, Tom. **Bike Tripping.** Illustrated by Rick Morrall. Clinton, MA: The Colonial Press, 1972. 161p, appendix, index, addresses.

The book is a complete guide to this popular leisure activity and includes chapters on learning to ride, which bike is best for the individual, safety, town cycling and country cycling, transporting bike and biker, tips for happy tripping, local bike trips, short country escape routes, tour trips, road racing trips, and extended bike trips.

Daitzman, Reid J. **Mental Jogging.** New York: Richard Marek Publishers, 1980. 216p and Selected Resources.

Designed for enjoyment, for stimulating the imagination, and for increasing problem and puzzle solving abilities, this book provides 365 games—one for each day in the year—for creative fun and mental exercise. The games have no "right" or "wrong" answers but multiple responses. They're more fun when played with one or several friends. The author contends that mental jogging is as important as physical jogging for achieving personal well-being. After each group of games, sample answers are listed for those who play the games to compare with how others have responded, thus opening more insights and ideas.

Greenberger, Ellen, and Laurence Steinberg. **When Teenagers Work: The Psychological and Social Costs of Adolescent Employment.** New York: Basic Books, Inc., 1986. 304p.

These researchers investigate adolescents in the workplace and observe the effects that can result from the experiences there. Many of their findings will surprise those who believe that work—any work—is good. This book will provide thought-provoking insights for teens and for parents who are considering work for their sons and daughters.

Halsted, Judith Wynn. **Guiding Gifted Readers from Preschool through High School.** Columbus: Ohio Psychology Publishing, 1988. 307p, bibliography.

Stressing the importance of using books for the intellectual and emotional development of gifted students, this handbook for parents, teachers, counselors, and librarians offers criteria for choosing texts and urges parents and educators to plan children's reading. The bibliography annotates 160 works.

Heltne, Paul G., and Linda A. Marquardt, eds. **Science Learning in the Informal Setting: Symposium Proceedings.** Chicago: Chicago Academy of Sciences, 1988. 337p.

This book is a collection of papers that discuss the role played by informal settings such as museums, parks, and zoos in advancing scientific literacy in people.

Henderson, Kathy. **Market Guide for Young Writers.** Shoe Tree, 1988. 171p.

This guide gives detailed information about markets and contests that welcome submissions from children and teenagers. The author spends two chapters telling how to select, prepare, and submit manuscripts as well as how to deal with rejections. A series of profiles of young writers shares their experiences and feelings with the readers. Additional sections include advice from professional editors, answers to most-often-asked questions, lists of resources, and a glossary.

**"High-Interest/Low-Reading-Level Booklist,"** compiled periodically by the Young Adult Services Division of the American Library Association.

The list includes both fiction and nonfiction books for teens who are reluctant to read. The titles should appeal to such potential readers in both interest and readability to encourage wider reading. This list and others are available for a small fee from YASD, ALA, 50 East Huron Street, Chicago, IL 60611. The interested person is asked to enclose a stamped, self-addressed envelope. Information is also available at libraries.

Lopez, Nancy, with Peter Schwed. **The Education of a Woman Golfer.** New York: Simon and Schuster, 1979. 188p.

This story of Nancy Lopez's life and career through her first, fabulous year is enhanced by photographs and illustrations. Lopez explains how she plays and how she feels about her major rivals and describes her golf education in terms of philosophy, biology, psychology, business, chemistry, and more.

Lyttle, Richard B. **The Complete Beginner's Guide to Backpacking.** Garden City, NY: Doubleday & Co., Inc., 1975. 136p, bibliography, index.

A comprehensive guide to backpacking, this handbook describes appropriate attitudes and conditioning for the activity as well as addresses the topics of equipment, skills, planning, and safety. Illustrated with photographs.

Man, John. **Walk! It Could Change Your Life.** New York and London: Paddington Press Ltd., 1979. 232p plus the Walker's Yellow Pages, suggested further reading, and four appendixes.

The author discusses topics such as walking versus running, walking and the heart, walking and weight loss, psychological and emotional benefits of walking; various types of walking, such as city, country, backpacking and rambling, nature, and race walking; and praises walking as fitness-promoting, not faddist, and without pressure-producing performance levels.

Patent, Dorothy Hinshaw. **The Quest for Artificial Intelligence.** San Diego, CA: Harcourt Brace Jovanovich, 1986. 187p.

Using diagrams, photographs, a bibliography for further reading, and a glossary, the author shows teens and adults how they can build on their common interest in computers. Topics include languages, games, robots, and expert systems such as those used in medical diagnoses. The author compares computers and the human brain and speculates on the nature of intelligence.

Portchmouth, John. **Creative Crafts for Today.** New York: The Viking Press, 1970. 180p plus suggested themes and topics and further reading.

Based on the premise that everyone is creative, the book gives the inquiring mind practical and comprehensive assistance in how to do crafts, where to find materials (such as scraps, plaster, jars, fishbones, eggshells, corks, clay, tree bark), what to use materials for, and how to design and make specific crafts.

The President's Council on Physical Fitness. **Get Fit.** Washington, DC: Department of Health and Human Services, 1987. 39p.

In an easy-to-read format, this booklet lists the keys to success in any undertaking, gives motivational tips for fitness, explains what fitness is and how it's measured, describes body composition, describes ways to improve, and gives the new presidential fitness award program and exercise program and a fitness quiz.

Richards, Norman. **The Complete Beginner's Guide to Soaring and Hang Gliding.** Garden City, NY: Doubleday & Co., Inc., 1976. 111p, glossary, appendix.

These two sports offer an exhilarating sense of achievement and hold a broad appeal. What's needed to get involved are an interest in the natural forces that make a sailplane or hang glider fly, says the author, and the ingenuity to take advantage of these elements along with the proper training to make it safe and enjoyable. The comprehensive, fully illustrated guide is for beginners of all ages.

Stodell, Ernestine. **Deep Song: The Dance Story of Martha Graham.** New York: Schirmer Books (Macmillan), 1984. 262p, epilogue, notes, bibliography, and chronology of works.

The author tells of Martha Graham's extraordinary struggle to bring her ideas to life and of the eventual triumph of her compulsive, intuitive, and disciplined personality through the symbolism of dance. The book portrays the dancer's personal and professional life from the time she was a young girl in Santa Barbara to her adulthood as a rebellious artist. Graham is said to have made a great contribution toward the advancement of the humanities.

Stone, William S. **A Guide to American Sports Car Racing.** Photographs by Martin J. Dain. Garden City, NY: Doubleday & Co., Inc., 1971. 206p. Bibliography, "Good Reading about Racing," and glossary.

Divided into four parts, part one, "What Goes on Here?" tells the history and organization of sports car racing, describes the course, explains the starts and straights and corners, and describes getting behind the wheel. Part two, "The Cars," describes the parts and makes of sports cars; part three is a portfolio of racing photos; and part four describes the various courses.

**"Summertime Favorites"** is a reading list collected by the National Endowment for the Humanities and published in the form of a free poster.

The list is based on a survey by the agency of supplemental reading lists provided by public and private schools and is limited to titles published in 1960 or before. Appropriate age levels are suggested. Copies are free by writing: "Summertime Favorites," Office of Publications and Public Affairs, National Endowment for the Humanities, 1100 Pennsylvania Ave., NW, Room 406, Washington, DC 20506.

# Nonprint Materials

**Balancing Act**
Type:     16mm film, sound
Length:   15 min.
Cost:     Free; borrower pays return postage; reserve in advance.

*Source:*    Modern Talking Picture Service
             Film Scheduling Center
             5000 Park Street, North
             St. Petersburg, FL 33709
*Date:*      1978

This film takes a timely, youthful approach to weight control
for teenagers through the concept of "calories in—calories
out," balancing food intake with energy output. The
important relationship of food and exercise is stressed with
humor and good sense.

**The CBS/Fox Guide to Home Videography**
*Type:*       Video
*Length:*     60 min.
*Cost:*       Purchase $29.95
*Title no.:*  S 00755
*Source:*     University of Illinois Film/Video Center
              1325 South Oak Street
              Champaign, IL 61820

This instructional tape guides amateur videographers from
the planning of a program to correct use of the home video
camera. It includes hints about framing, composition,
lighting, and sound.

**Keep It in Balance**
*Type:*       16mm film, sound
*Length:*     15 min.
*Cost:*       Free; borrower pays return postage and insurance.
*Source:*     Film Community
              West Glen Films
              1430 Broadway, 9th Floor
              New York, NY 10018

A group of high school students, unimpressed by a film on
nutrition, are challenged by their teacher to make their own
movies. In interviews with professionals for the project,
they're shown the hazards of fad diets and learn they can eat
a variety of foods as long as they balance intake with proper
exercise. Available only in AL, AZ, CA, CO, ID, IL, IA, KS,
MN, MO, MT, NE, NV, ND, NM, OK, OR, SD, northwest TX,
UT, WA, WI, WY.

### Learning Photography from Kodak Series

*Type:* Video, 4 in the series
*Length:* 45 min. each tape
*Cost:* Purchase $14.95 each or $49.95 for the 4-volume set
*Title no.:* S 02326
*Source:* University of Illinois Film/Video Center
1325 South Oak Street
Champaign, IL 61820

The series covers basic comprehensive information for the amateur photographer, giving tips and techniques for better pictures.

### The Searching Eye

*Type:* 16mm film, color
*Length:* 18 min.
*Source:* Pyramid Films
Box 1048
Santa Monica, CA 90406

Winner of the Grand Award, Venice International Children's Film Festival, this film produced by Saul Bass and Associates for the Eastman Kodak Company stresses the importance of the art of seeing—the skill of probing and understanding the surrounding world—as one of the most important goals of learning. The film stresses that the art of seeing involves using all the senses. Using minimum narration, the film presents a simple sequence of a boy exploring and playing on the beach. By understatement a larger message is revealed of how experience and years teach the eye to contemplate the unknown and find meaning.

### Ski the Outer Limits

*Type:* 16mm film, color
*Length:* 27 min.
*Source:* Pyramid Films
Box 1048
Santa Monica, CA 90406

This double award winner at the American Film Festival shows a graceful series of skiing sequences, including skiers somersaulting, professional competitions, and both young and old learning the fundamentals of skiing with comic episodes to relieve the discomforts of learning. A middle-aged skier is photographed still challenging the snow and testing the outer limits of his capabilities. The effect on the viewer is one of exhilaration and a fresh appreciation of the sport and how the message can be applied to one's own life.

## Why Man Creates

Type:      16 mm film, color
Length:    25 min.
Source:    Pyramid Films
           Box 1048
           Santa Monica, CA 90406

Written by Saul Bass and Mayo Simon, this classic film has won numerous awards. It explores the nature of creativity in a series of eight separate but related sequences: "The Edifice," "Fooling Around: Sometimes Ideas Start That Way," "The Process," "The Judgment," "A Parable," "A Digression," "The Search," and "The Mark." The impact on the viewer is to feel the process of creating and to see it in a variety of ways. Bass believes in the development of the imagination as a vital aspect of both learning and of becoming human.

## The World of Remote Control

Type:       Video
Length:     22 min.
Cost:       Purchase $39.95
Title no.:  S 01853
Source:     University of Illinois Film/Video Center
            1325 South Oak Street
            Champaign, IL 61820

This video explains how to pick a model and get started on the fascinating hobby of remote control. Opening with a montage of every type of vehicle that can be powered and steered by remote control, the video then describes equipment needed and how it operates. It explains the roles of transmitter, receiver, servos, and batteries and includes boats, cars, and model jet airplanes.

# Organizations

### American Youth Work Center (AYWC)
1522 Connecticut Avenue, NW, 4th Floor
Washington, DC 20036
(202) 785-0764
*Executive Director: William W. Treanor*

The Center represents the interests of community-based
youth service programs, including group homes, runaway
programs, counseling centers, hotlines, multipurpose
programs, youth employment programs, and delinquency
treatment and prevention programs. It helps with youth
service programs through training, seminars, technical
assistance, conferences, legislative information, and research.
It is an advocate for youth programs and monitors Congress
and federal agencies as well as coordinates international
exchange programs for youth workers. The Center maintains
a speakers' bureau.

PUBLICATIONS: *National Directory of Runaway Programs*,
biennial; also publishes books, studies, and pamphlets.
Holds an annual convention/meeting.

### Boy Scouts of America (BSA)
1325 Walnut Hill Lane
Irving, TX 75038
(214) 580-2000
*Chief Scout Executive: Ben H. Love*

Divisions of BSA include Tiger Cubs, age 6; Cub Scouts, ages
7–10; Boy Scouts, ages 11–18; Explorers (male and female),
ages 15–20; Lone Scouts; male and female adult leaders and
volunteer workers. Programs are offered through community-
based religious, civic, and educational groups. It encourages
in-school scouting and offers religious emblems created by
major church denominations. BSA operates councils and
districts in local communities; maintains a museum and
library of 8,000 volumes related to social studies, youth
work, and history; compiles statistics; sponsors competitions;
and bestows awards including post–high school scholarships.
The club's purpose is for character development, citizenship

training, and physical and mental fitness for boys and young adults.

PUBLICATIONS: *Boys' Life,* monthly; *Scouting Magazine* (for adults), 6/year; *Exploring Magazine* (for Explorers), 4/year; *Annual Report to Congress;* also publishes handbooks and manuals for Boy Scouts, Cub Scouts, Explorers, and adult leaders; merit badge pamphlets; and more than 2,000 BSA program items. Affiliated with World Scout Bureau and holds a biennial convention/meeting.

**Camp Fire, Inc. (CFI)**
4601 Madison Avenue
Kansas City, MO 64112
(816) 756-1950
*Executive Director: David W. Bahlmann*

Local groups include girls and boys up to 21 years of age. Purpose is to provide, through a program of informal education, opportunities for youth to realize their potential and to function effectively as caring, self-directed individuals, responsible to themselves and to others. Activities focus on small-group learning by doing; developing a positive self-image; responsibility and creativity; gaining decision-making and planning skills; and learning to appreciate, care about, and work with others. It sponsors community and collaborative events for youths, makes awards, and conducts research and compiles statistics. Clubs include Adventure, Blue Birds, Discovery, Horizon, and Sparks.

PUBLICATIONS: *Camp Fire Management,* 9/year; *Leadership Magazine,* 3/year; *Annual Report;* and also publishes manuals, youth program books, leader guide books, pamphlets, and other materials. Biennial congress convention/meeting is held.

**Delta Teen-Lift (Travel) (DTL)**
Delta Sigma Theta, Inc.
1707 New Hampshire Avenue, NW
Washington, DC 20009
(202) 483-5460
*Program Director: Ella McNair*

A number of local groups are sponsored by Delta Sigma
Theta to raise the aspirations of disadvantaged teenagers by
providing travel experiences that combine first-hand
information about educational opportunities and facilities,
contact with persons in diversified occupations, and an
opportunity to meet and talk with people who have made
outstanding contributions to public and private enterprises.
Teen-Lift takes selected young people on organized tours to
educational, business, and cultural centers in metropolitan
areas and is sponsored by Delta Sigma Theta sorority.

PUBLICATIONS: *Delta,* periodic newsletter; *Delta Journal,*
periodic journal. Biennial convention/meeting with exhibits.

### 4-H Program (4-H)
Extension Service
U.S. Department of Agriculture
Washington, DC 20250
(202) 447-5853
*Deputy Administrator: Dr. Donald Stormer*

Members of 4-H groups range from 9 to 19 years of age, in
rural and urban areas of almost all counties in the United
States, Puerto Rico, Guam, Virgin Islands, and the District of
Columbia. Volunteer adult and junior leaders guide activities
designed to foster character development and good citizenship through a wide variety of projects emphasizing the
objectives of 4-H. The program is part of the national
educational system of cooperative extension work shared by
the U.S. Department of Agriculture, state land-grant
universities, and counties with the national and state
extension services providing leadership.

PUBLICATIONS: *4-H Leader,* monthly. Affiliated with
National 4-H Council and holds annual National 4-H
Conference and annual National 4-H Week.

### Girl Scouts of the U.S.A. (GSUSA)
830 Third Avenue and 51st Street
New York, NY 10022
(212) 940-7500
*Executive Director: Frances R. Hesselbein*

Local groups include several for younger girls; Cadette Girl
Scouts for ages 12–14; Senior Girl Scouts, for ages 14–17.

The purpose is "to help girls develop as happy, resourceful individuals willing to share their abilities as citizens in their homes, their communities, their country and the world." Its program encourages self-awareness, interaction with others, development of values, and service to society and provides girls with opportunities to expand personal interests, learn new skills, and explore career possibilities. It also offers leadership training, international exchange programs, and conferences and seminars on a variety of topics. Maintains library and archives.

PUBLICATIONS: *GSUSA News,* monthly; *Girl Scout Leader,* 4/year; *Annual Environmental Scanning Report; Annual Report.* Affiliated with World Association of Girl Guides and Girl Scouts and sponsors a triennial convention/meeting with exhibits.

**National Network of Youth Advisory Boards (NNYAB)**
P.O. Box 402036, Ocean View Branch
Miami Beach, FL 33140
(305) 532-2607
*Executive Director: Stuart Alan Rado*

The Network is composed of youth service bureaus, community action agencies, youth advisory boards, juvenile justice programs, schools, and other youth programs. It promotes youth participation in the decision-making process and in youth programs in areas such as education, employment, drug and alcohol abuse, recreation, and juvenile justice. It provides technical assistance to help community leaders establish youth participation councils or advisory boards and promotes seminars and conferences, resource identification, and program networking. Maintains 500-volume library.

PUBLICATIONS: Newsletter, quarterly; also publishes follow-up reports.

**Outward Bound**
384 Gield Point Road
Greenwich, CT 06830
(203) 661-0797
*President: John F. Reynolds III*

The organization operates five schools in the United States
to help men and women discover and extend their own
resources and abilities by confronting them with a series of
increasingly difficult challenges in a wilderness setting. Each
school offers courses from 4 to 30 days in length that include
physical conditioning, technical training, team training,
expeditions, and community service to foster the educational
development of the total human. The group provides
financial aid to about one-third of its participants and offers
substance abuse, mental health, and managers' courses, and
courses for youth at risk and has assisted in establishing a
training program for Peace Corps volunteers.

PUBLICATIONS: Outward Bound catalog and report, annual;
irregular newsletters; and the book *Outward Bound USA*.

### REACH—Responsible Educated Adolescents Can Help (Drug Abuse)
c/o Denise Bozick
14950 444th Avenue, SE
North Bend, WA 98045
(206) 888-0278
*Executive Director: Denise Bozick*

This is an organization of teenagers working to end drug
abuse among young people. It received national attention as
part of an anti-drug ceremony held by former first lady
Nancy Reagan. The group is affiliated with the National
Federation of Parents for Drug-Free Youth. (Source: *The
Washington Post*, 23 February 1985.)

### Youth of All Nations (YOAN)
16 St. Luke's Place
New York, NY 10014
(212) 924-1358
*Executive Associate: Anita Leiser*

This organization is for persons between ages 14 and 24 who
want to correspond with young adults in other nations. Its
purpose is to help young people understand and appreciate
other nations and cultures, "thus deepening insights into
their own." Members are put in touch with others and given

a booklet of suggestions on how to begin and maintain a correspondence. Requests for information in the United States should include a stamped, self-addressed return envelope and 25 cents. The group maintains a library. Nominated for the Nobel Peace Prize in 1979 and the W. Averell Harriman Distinguished International Service Award in 1983.

PUBLICATIONS: *Mirror for Youth,* irregular; also distributes booklet of correspondence hints to members.

## U.S.-U.S.S.R. Partnerships
Room 530
1619 Massachusetts Avenue, NW
Washington, DC 20036
(202) 328-7309

This organization's purpose is to arrange exchange high school experiences, both public and nonpublic, for students with proficiency in the Russian language. The group forms a partnership between schools and is run by the National Association of Secondary School Principals, the American Council of Teachers of Russian, and Sister Cities International.

## Youth for Christ/U.S.A. (YFC/USA)
Carol Stream
360 South Main Place
Wheaton, IL 60189
(312) 668-6600
*Executive Officer: Gary Dausey*

This interdenominational organization is for the evangelization and discipling of teenagers. It fights juvenile delinquency through counseling and programs for youth penal institutions, carries on projects in 62 countries through its international organization, and maintains a placement service. Programs for youth include camps, campus life, clubs, conferences, counseling, youth guidance work with troubled teenagers. "Family Forum" airs on 230 radio stations daily. It has a number of departments and divisions and holds a triennial winter teen conference and a triennial summer regional conference.

**Youth Office, Organization of American States (OAS)**
1889 F Street
Washington, DC 20006
(202) 789-3000
*Contact: Roberto Scioville*

Member countries are those in the Organization of American States with the goal to provide financial and material support for youth-oriented programs. It provides assistance to governing arms of youth programs, which include federal agencies, private foundations, and OAS offices overseas. The main activity is to sponsor youth conferences focusing on such topics as international law, agriculture and technology, and handicapped persons. It promotes educational and sports activities for young people.

# CHAPTER 5

# Getting Help

"Why are you so upset?" Mr. Hewitt said. He spoke all the more kindly.

Alex hunched his shoulders and lips again, as if not knowing or not wanting to say.

"Something at home?"

"Nah," Alex said.

"I know you've missed a lot of school lately. What have you been doing? I'm not going to punish you or anything. Perhaps I can help."

"Ah, just a lot of bad things," Alex said. But his voice failed to work clearly.

> Theodore Weesner, *The Car Thief* (New
> York: Dell Publishing, 1973 [1967]), 24.

Alex, in Theodore Weesner's novel, falls into bad company and gets into trouble with the law as a car thief. His personal problems in turn create problems at school. Fear, lack of confidence in himself, the deep need for acceptance and approval, combine with other elements that make it difficult for Alex to concentrate on schoolwork.

When his teacher treats him kindly and with genuine concern, Alex doesn't know how to respond appropriately. Later in the story, he wants to date Irene; but even though she, too, treats him with kindness and warmth, he lacks the confidence to tell her he'd like to spend time with her. Again, he can't concentrate on what's going on in school because he's trying to work out his feelings about Irene and to resolve his trouble with the law. With his inner turmoil, he's torn between fear of showing up at school and fear of what can happen if he doesn't show up.

---

People of whatever learning ability or chronological point in their school years—even just six weeks before they're due to graduate—may reach a point when they feel they can't face school one more day. So they drop out. And dropping out means they face a whole new set of problems.

Most people have the resilience to bounce back, figure out a solution or a plan of action, and keep going when difficulties arise or when things don't turn out as expected. But when problems persist or pile up, the tension begins to take its toll, both on the students themselves and on how they're doing in school. When that happens, it's time to stop, identify the problem, try to find the source of the trouble, and figure out how to get help and look for options.

When people either know or feel that things aren't working out the way they should at school, some places they can look for help include:

> *School and public libraries.* Libraries stock numerous self-help books, pamphlets, and other materials that list other places to explore as possible sources for help. Usually such books take a practical approach, using a clearly structured format that makes it easy to follow the suggested steps or to choose parts that apply and eliminate the ones that don't. *Book stores,* too, carry inexpensive self-help publications. And librarians and bookstore employees are eager to help people find exactly the right materials.

> *School guidance and counseling offices.* Knowledgeable counselors who are good listeners can offer helpful information or refer students to other appropriate sources of help. They also either have on hand or can recommend pamphlets, books, and tapes on the subjects of a student's concern.

*Teachers.* Many teachers, like the one in the chapter's opening quotation, are truly concerned about their students' well-being and can offer help similar to what a strong guidance counselor can give. The advantage of a teacher for some students is that they've developed familiarity and trust with someone they see daily, while the counselor is someone they see only occasionally. For some it's easier to talk with someone familiar; others find it easier to talk with someone they don't know so well.

*Family members* (parents, siblings, grandparents, aunts, uncles, cousins). People in the family know one another's history and personality. They can give general advice and offer special insights into particular family member behaviors that might help the young person gain a more comprehensive understanding of the situation and of how to work it out.

*Family doctor.* If there's a chance the situation may be caused by a health or medical problem, the family doctor is the right person to see. But that doctor can also give sympathetic, practical help for emotional and social issues the young person finds confusing or distressing.

*A minister, rabbi, or priest.* These religious leaders have training, knowledge, and experience in counseling and can often give practical as well as spiritual help to people.

*Community mental and physical health clinics.* For either emotional or physical concerns, public health clinics provide people even on limited incomes the advice and counseling they seek. These days most persons at least once in their lives need the objective, knowledge-able, and useful help of professionals to ease emotional distress such as loss, grief, fear, or confusion. Society has grown so complex that everyone needs help at times to sort things out and get back onto a clear track. It's important to get a personality match between counselor or doctor and the person asking for help.

*Community support groups.* People sharing a similar problem—such as death of a close family member, some form of addiction, a food disorder, or a physical problem—get together on a regular basis to share their common trials and successes and to lend moral support to one another in setting and keeping goals.

*Peers.* Often others in the same age group have experienced similar problems and are willing to talk about how they handled the situation. It's often less inhibiting to talk with those about the same age than it is with older adults. Peers seem less judgmental, and just talking with someone who listens empathetically can help a confused or troubled person find his or her own answers.

*Tutoring services, at school or privately.* When school-work is the problem, or even before it becomes a problem, tutoring one-on-one can catch the student up to speed with the rest of the class or at least enough to gain a working knowledge of what's required.

*Older students or recent graduates.* Because these individuals are still close to many experiences the troubled person may be having, their fresh recall can provide detailed help others may overlook. They also tend to be a more sympathetic audience.

## If School Is the Problem

When it's the situation at school that seems to be the source of the student's difficulty, some things to try before making a decision to drop out could include

Asking for a transfer to another school within reasonable distance

Arranging to live in another community with a family friend or relative in order to attend a new school there

For a public school student, exploring private school options and finding out about financial help to pay tuition there

If none of these suggestions fits, a student may decide to leave school. Before that, though, she needs to be aware that she's closing doors that will be difficult if not impossible to open again. One option for a high school dropout, the General Educational Development (GED) certificate, can substitute for a high school diploma in getting certain jobs as well as in going on to some colleges, trade, or vocational schools. But the military services no longer accept people with GED's, so that option will be closed, along with a variety of others. In some cases, though, the GED may be the best answer for getting on with life.

Some dropouts opt to get a job, and then enroll in night school to complete work for a diploma in order to qualify for more desirable positions or simply to fill in what they feel they've missed by leaving school. Other students who drop out come back to school, sometimes a year later, with the determination to get all they can out of their studies and earn their high school diplomas.

## When Attitude Causes Problems

Sometimes the problem hinges on attitude. Without a positive outlook, belief in self, the willingness to work hard and be open-minded and nurture the desire to learn, school seems futile. Some ways to pull out of a negative attitude can include finding a new hobby or interest, having a change of scene or taking a needed break from the routine, making a new friend, seeing a happy movie, or reading a fascinating novel. Some people get their anger or hurt out by cleaning out all the drawers and closets or polishing the car. Finding constructive ways to vent feelings arms people to face life at school again with stronger confidence and purpose. Trying to focus on the long-term benefits that come from staying in school strengthens the urge to tolerate or try to improve an undesirable home or school situation.

When students find themselves thinking that school has nothing to offer or that they'll take from school only those things that make life more pleasant, then they are cheating themselves of what they could get out of school with a different attitude and point of view. To change their attitudes, they can help themselves by making friends with people who have a positive outlook and who support them in their efforts to change. Because most people tend to think mainly in terms of present satisfaction, it's not so easy to foresee how things that happen today affect the direction of the future.

Another great enemy of learning is apathy. For a variety of reasons, some students fail to see the need to learn or to exert their energies to do what's expected of them at school. Without the desire to learn, students are bound to have problems.

But most people also have the desire to stretch themselves, to take on new challenges, and to discover and develop the talents that lie within them. Scott Thomson, executive director of the National Association of Secondary School Principals (NASSP), said that "Students need to be motivated to achieve, to accept the toughest challenges, to strive to learn" (9). When they do that, they raise their self-esteem, even if it takes a while to succeed or if they fail. People need to experience failure to understand that only through failure can learning successfully occur.

In a true story written by Pulitzer Prize–winning journalist Jon Franklin, a neurosurgeon takes on the challenge of a formidable piece of brain surgery. Just when he thinks he may have succeeded in extracting the "monster" tumor in his patient's brain, a surprise twist in the situation hands the victory to the monster rather than to Dr. Ducker; the surgery fails and the patient dies. The surgeon feels disappointed, defeated. But the failure doesn't devastate him. He knows that he will fail in other surgery attempts, too, as his career proceeds, but that what he has learned in performing this piece of surgery could give him the information he needs to succeed in a similar operation later. Dr. Ducker does not allow failure to destroy his spirit and his will. He holds onto his positive attitude and his self-esteem. He understands that in the challenges of his profession, as in those of life, he'll "win some and he'll lose some." He focuses on the wins, not the losses.

A Pennsylvania journalism teacher, Alex Gruenberg, wrote about a bright female student whose performance as a sophomore disappointed him. But when he assigned an article on a topic that challenged her curiosity, she became highly motivated and carried out the project with thoroughness and quality. He compared this girl's problem with that shared by unlikely peers—"the ones who skip school frequently, or sleep in class, or who come in high or hung over. The ones who disrupt. The ones who drop out. The ones who die." He explained that what these students shared in common was the fact that they didn't feel very good about themselves. "They lack motivation, self-confidence, and resiliency. They have poor self-esteem." And although these students had other problems, too, the school newspaper advisor said he believed the lack of self-esteem to be the root problem (15).

These and other examples clearly show that holding on to self-esteem and the motivation to learn isn't easy. Part of the reason is that parents and teachers (and students themselves) tend to focus on the weaknesses rather than the strengths of the young people they care about. When the negative rather than the positive is emphasized, the negative takes over a person's emotional self. One way to counteract the hammering of repeated negative messages is for individuals to take a few minutes at the end of each day to write a list of things enjoyed that day, things they succeeded in doing (including getting a smile out of someone who doesn't ordinarily smile), and things they like about themselves. While everyone wants approval, the most important approval of all is self-approval. When all the outside expressions of praise are just echoes in the memory, the person who won that praise honestly can give himself a hearty pat on the back for his praiseworthy performance. Or when public reaction is negative, but the student feels she's stayed true to her personal belief and value system, she can cheer her courage in standing against the crowd.

## When Things at Home Get Out of Focus

Family situations these days are not so clearly defined as they once were. Many young people experience more emotional stress at home. They may live in homes where their parents fight; or the parents are divorced, and the teenagers are dividing themselves between two entirely different sets of home environments and expectations, or they are living with a family that's a combination of a stepparent and a biological parent, and one or more stepsiblings and biological siblings. Moreover, in many families both parents work. That means high school students are on their own, more so than those in previous generations, and in some cases teenagers are responsible for doing household tasks or caring for younger brothers and sisters. Many families relocate frequently, meaning each family member has to adjust to changes with each move.

Some homes are under financial pressures or a family member has a health problem, or a parent is an alcoholic or the victim of some other kind of addictive behavior. In such homes, young people lose out on their most basic support system. Some eventually leave home either voluntarily or because their parents tell them to leave. That means they're out on their own before they have the maturity or experience to take on that responsibility. Yet many young people do it successfully; others walk into serious, destructive situations.

## Family Communication as a Problem

But communication between teenagers and their parents has long been a problem in many homes, traditional or nontraditional. Paul Zindel's novels and plays often depict that problem. For example, in Zindel's novel *The Pigman*, John makes an all-out effort to explain to his father how he feels about wanting to discover the kind of future career that's right for him. He thinks he's done a pretty fair job of getting his point across. But he knows his father hasn't really listened when the response he gets is

> "Be yourself! Be individualistic! ... But for God's sake get your hair cut. You look like an oddball." (68)

Often high school students rely on their friends as the only people who will really listen to them. In *The Pigman*, John finds a nonjudgmental listener in a lonely old widower, Mr. Pignati. In many cases grandparents can become the trusted confidantes of high school students because their experience gives them greater insight and objectivity in seeing the young person's point of view. If attempts of parents and teens to communicate fail, they may need to give each other "space" for a period of time.

Because it's difficult to communicate individual needs most people don't experience, a young person who is "different"—handicapped, of minority race or religion, different lifestyle, or gifted—will encounter conflicts and problems. The young artist in Chaim Potok's novel *My Name Is Asher Lev* experiences personal, family, and community problems because he's gifted. It is excruciatingly painful for Asher Lev to conform to what is expected of him at school and at home. He knows he is hurting those he loves when he follows his own compulsion to be an artist. So he tries to please his parents and teachers while continuing to do what he must as an artist. He does only the minimum to get by in school, but is passionate in his pursuit of art. Gifted athletes, musicians, scientists, or persons with a special talent can identify with Asher Lev's inner conflict when a religious leader who is a friend of the family says:

> Many people feel they are in possession of a great gift
> when they are young. But one does not always give in
> to the gift. One does with a life what is precious not
> only to one's own self but one's own people. (128)

The older man forces the younger one to choose between two values, both precious to his life. The older one, set in his own belief of what is right, cannot listen to the younger one's need. The reverse can also be true in other situations.

Home problems affect how a student does in school. But that effect can be either positive or negative. Sometimes when things are bad at home, the student can forget his troubles at school and concentrate on life within the school walls, finding relief from the home pressures and a means of surviving the home problems. On the other hand, some students may be so overcome by problems at home that they find it impossible to concentrate at school. These students need professional help and may even need to move out of the home.

When people reach the point where they need help, they're impatient to get results. But serious problems build over a long period of time. They won't disappear overnight. As Carl Sandburg in his poem "What Shall He Tell That Son?" wrote, "A tough will counts" (56).

# REFERENCES

Franklin, Jon. "Mrs. Kelly's Monster." *Writing for Story.* New York: A Mentor Book, New American Library, 1986.

Gruenberg, Alex. "Self-esteem: Another Justification for Publication." *The Dow Jones Newspaper Fund Advisor Update*, Princeton, NJ (Summer 1989): 15.

Potok, Chaim. *My Name Is Asher Lev.* New York: A Fawcett Crest Book, 1972.

Sandburg, Carl. "What Shall He Tell That Son?" *I've Got A Name.* Ed. by Charlotte Brooks and Lawana Trout. New York: Holt, Rinehart and Winston, 1968. 56.

Thomson, Scott. "Teachers Should Set Higher Goals So Students Will Be Successful." Reston, VA. Printed in *The Fort Morgan Times*, 3 May 1988: 9.

Weesner, Theodore. *The Car Thief.* New York: Dell Publishing, 1973 [1967].

Zindel, Paul. *The Pigman.* New York: Dell Publishing, 1968.

# Resources

## Fiction

Arrick, Fran. **Nice Girl from Good Home.** New York: Dell Publishing, 1986 [1984]. 192p.

When 15-year-old Dory Hewitt's father loses his well-paying job and finds he's overqualified for available jobs, each family member reacts in different ways to their drastically changed circumstances. Dory rebels, skips school, and becomes a troublemaker. Her 17-year-old brother Jeremy copes. The actions of the two teenagers, their friends, and parents dramatize different ways of reacting to the changed circumstances. Readers observe solutions that work and those that don't.

Cross, Gillian. **A Map of Nowhere.** New York: Holiday House, 1989. 150p.

Nick is enticed enough by the idea of gang membership to join and gets into trouble that makes him decide what his values really are. This fascinating fantasy/science fiction novel provokes serious discussions about the similarities between game quests and those challenges that shape painful choices in real life.

Crutcher, Chris. **The Crazy Horse Electric Game.** New York: Greenwillow/Morrow, 1987. 215p.

Sixteen-year-old Willie Weaver's chances for success at his new high school are slight. Badly injured after a water-skiing accident, he has run away from his misunderstanding parents and friends, been robbed by a street gang, and rescued by a bus driver. The bus driver sends him to the new school, where Willie, by trying hard and practicing Tai Chi, recovers his health and makes it in the new school. Later, returning home, he discovers that the family has disintegrated.

Evans, Shirlee. **A Life in Her Hands.** Scottdale, PA: Herald, 1987. 188p.

Fifteen and pregnant, Gail is scared. Her foster parents and their minister advise her to enter a home for pregnant teens, where Gail shares the lives and hardships of other girls. She finally decides to place her child for adoption. While the book may seem a bit on the preachy side, it addresses some aspects of this situation that most books don't. Pregnancy is one of the major reasons girls drop out of school. Watching what happens to Gail can show readers the consequences of decisions that affect the directions of their lives.

Guest, Judith. **Ordinary People.** New York: Ballantine Books, 1976. 245p.

This popular novel, also a movie, dramatizes a high school boy's depression and guilt following his older brother's accidental drowning. Conrad struggles to lead an ordinary life like that of his classmates in between regular visits to the psychologist—visits that unnerve Conrad with their probing of his emotional conflicts. His adjustment and acceptance are complicated by the breakup of his parents' marriage. But Conrad is helped by a new friendship with romantic potential. The story helps readers understand themselves and others better and to understand also how emotional problems affect the ability to focus on schoolwork.

Janeczko, Paul B. **Bridges to Cross.** New York: Macmillan, 1986. 168p.

James Marchuk struggles to adjust when his mother insists he attend a religious high school instead of public school. He feels that the school and his mother's rigid rules are suffocating him. Finally, James's mother comes to realize she has to give him room to find his own individuality. The novel dramatizes how the problem of communication between parent and young person can create hard feelings at home and make the young person's life at school unpleasant as well.

LeGuin, Ursula. **Very Far Away from Anywhere Else.** New York: Bantam Books, 1978 [1976]. 87p.

LeGuin's novel depicts how two young people, Owen and Natalie, drawn together because they are outsiders at school, build a special loyalty, joy, and friendship. Both gifted, one wants to be a great scientist, the other a musician, and they pursue those goals with passion and with one another's support. Because they don't let what their peers seem to feel about them damage their self-images, they're able to get the most out of both school and their life goal pursuits.

Peyton, K. M. **Pennington's Last Term.** New York: Harper and Row, 1979. 216p.

Patrick Pennington, bored with five years in high school, is badgered by his headmaster to cut his long hair. He also gets into trouble with the police. Rebelling against the arbitrariness of authority, Penn unexpectedly finds meaning for his life in his music and his ability to play piano.

Potok, Chaim. **My Name Is Asher Lev.** New York: A Fawcett Crest Book, 1972. 350p.

Asher Lev, a young artistically gifted boy, works to cope with his impatience with school and with adults who have his "best" interests in mind. At the same time he takes advantage of every opportunity to satisfy the compelling drive within him to use his artistic talent.

Richardson, Grace. **Douglas.** New York: Harper and Row, 1966. 230p.

Doug McPhillips has charm, easy intelligence, and enthusiasm but gets expelled from McKenzie Hall (thus losing his scholarship) and from junior high. At McGill University his musical and artistic talents win him friends, but he can't stick to any project and is forever disappointing family, friends, and his music teacher. Through continuing loyalty from friends and his sister's help, he at last faces the weakness in his character and resolves to earn not only their friendship but their respect.

Richmond, Sandra. **Wheels for Walking.** New York: Signet/NAL, 1988. 165p.

Sally, a promising life ahead of her, is left a quadriplegic after a tragic car accident. Sally lashes out in anger at everyone. It's her natural reaction to her loss of a sense of dignity and self-worth. Gradually her therapist and her counselor help her to accept herself as she is and strive for independence. Only when she regains some feelings of self-worth can she continue with educational and other goals.

Savitz, Harriet May. **On the Move.** New York: Avon, 1973. 123p.

The Zippers are a wheelchair basketball team with great courage, strength, and skill. The members of that team dramatize different personalities and their ways of coping with their physical handicap. Among the fans are another young person in a wheelchair, Carrie Davis, and her "walkie" sister. Through her friendships with members of the team and other wheelchair people, Carrie at last gains the will to attain her independence and lead a life of her own.

Ure, Jean. **You Win Some, You Lose Some.** New York: Dell Publishing, 1988. 201p.

This book helps shatter the myth of the stereotypical male ballet dancer. It is about a young man whose performance at school and on the soccer team are mediocre and whose ambition is to become a ballet dancer. Jamie leaves school, moves to London—hoping to get into a ballet academy—and balances a department-store job with grueling dance lessons. His rigorous schedule leaves little time for Jamie's other obsession—finding a girlfriend. The witty dialogue and interesting characters appeal to a wide reading audience.

White, Ellen Emerson. **Life Without Friends.** Englewood Cliffs, NJ: Scholastic, 1987. 250p.

High school senior Beverly Johnson has no friends. She blames herself for the deaths of two fellow students, has an ambivalent relationship with her father, and resents her stepmother. But when she meets Derek, he helps her accept her past and rebuild her self-image. Friendship helps her cope with school and other aspects of her life.

# Nonfiction

Colgrove, Melba, Ph.D., Harold H. Bloomfield, M.D., and Peter McWilliams. **How To Survive the Loss of a Love.** New York: Bantam Books, 1981 [1976]. 119p.

The format of the book makes it easy to read one to three pages at a time on a specific aspect of loss. Readers are taken through the experience of losing (even the missing of a telephone call), surviving, healing, and growing. The authors point out that there are all kinds of losses, the obvious and the not-so-obvious, and describe the feelings of loss and the stages of recovery.

Eagen, Andrea Boroff. **Why Am I So Miserable If These Are the Best Years of My Life?** New York: Avon, 1979 [1976]. 210p, additional and recommended reading.

The author offers practical wisdom about the things that concern young women as they grow up, including the body and how to care for it, relationships with boys as friends and as boyfriends, relationships with others (girlfriends, parents, teachers, adults in general), and about legal rights. The book was named an American Library Association–YASD (Young Adult Services Division) Best Book of the Year and the *School Library Journal* Best Book of the Year. Understanding and accepting what's happening to them as they mature can help young women feel more comfortable with themselves and hence be better able to concentrate on their work at school.

Miller, Gordon Porter. **Life Choices.** New York: Bantam Books, 1981. 166p.

Subtitled *How to Make Decisions, Take Control of Your Life,
and Get the Future You Want,* this useful book shows
readers a step-by-step approach to being a decision maker.
The author describes such concepts as discovering what
choices are open, analyzing risks and rewards, using
information and advice effectively, learning to set and meet
goals, conquering procrastination, coping with pressure
from others, and being confident when faced with a decision.
The purpose of the book is to help readers get more out
of life, a goal that also helps the person get more out of
school.

Schowalter, John E., M.D., and Walter R. Anyan, M.D. **The
Family Handbook of Adolescence.** New York: Alfred A.
Knopf, 1979. 303p.

The authors, a professional psychologist and a pediatrician,
have made this most readable book a source of reliable basic
information about questions young people, their parents,
and their teachers may ask about the years between 10 and
20 from a medical perspective. The authors explain all the
common physical, social, and psychological problems that
occur in the lives of teenagers. Appropriate places in the
book describe symptoms and treatments and whether an
ailment should be regarded as serious. The quick reference
style gives maximum usefulness for both teens and parents.
The book includes a section on how health relates to school
performance.

Wirths, Claudine G., and Mary Bowman-Kruhm. **I Hate
School: How To Hang In and When To Drop Out.** New York:
Crowell, 1986. 128p.

The book's seven chapters discuss what students who hate
school can do to make the experience more bearable. It
covers homework, reading, remembering, report writing, test
taking, and getting help. The book offers no promises but
warns students against following the crowd. It urges readers
not to give up asking for help because somewhere, if they
keep searching, there's someone who can help them.

# Nonprint Materials

## Behind Closed Doors

*Type:*      Video
*Length:*    30 min.
*Cost:*      Purchase $185
*Title no.:*  CC-857-VS
*Source:*    Human Relations Media
             Room CC
             175 Tompkins Avenue
             Pleasantville, NY 10570-9973

This video presents the real stories of teens who have lived through family problems and found ways to make them better. A teenage girl relates her efforts to break up the new family when her mom remarries. Another family talks frankly about the problem of sexual abuse and the steps they finally took to change. These stories can help viewers in need break out of their isolation and show them a path to recovery. A final segment on runaways in Los Angeles offers possible ways out of that difficulty.

## Confidence

*Type:*      Video
*Length:*    30 min.
*Cost:*      Purchase $24.95
*Title no.:*  ADLFM000102
*Source:*    Critics' Choice Video
             800 Morse Avenue
             Elk Grove Village, IL 60007

Teens can learn through this video how to overcome their hesitations, fears, and self-imposed limits in order to be the best they can be and do well in life.

## Drugs, Your Friends and You: Handling Peer Pressure

*Type:*      Video
*Length:*    26 min.
*Cost:*      Purchase $165
*Title no.:*  CC-2254-VS

*Source:* Human Relations Media
Room CC
175 Tompkins Avenue
Pleasantville, NY 10570-9973

The program makes students aware that they do have choices and that despite pressure from others, they can respect their own best interests and resist. The video helps teens make decisions against substance abuse, and then teaches specific techniques for dealing assertively with pro-drug/alcohol pressures.

### Fitting In: A New Look at Peer Pressure

*Type:* Video
*Length:* 25 min.
*Cost:* Purchase $165
*Title no.:* CC-5024-VS
*Source:* Human Relations Media
Room CC
175 Tompkins Avenue
Pleasantville, NY 10570-9973

The program is designed to unite teenagers in understanding the nature of peer pressure. It provides them with the tools and skills they may use to handle negative peer pressure, provides some positive steps toward building self-esteem, and shows how to promote positive peer pressure.

### The Healing Force

*Type:* Video
*Length:* 76 min.
*Cost:* Purchase $14.95
*Source:* Critics' Choice Video
800 Morse Avenue
Elk Grove Village, IL 60007

Author Norman Cousins reveals the secrets that laughter, love, and positive thinking possess and how they can add years of enjoyment to a person's life. The presentation is winner of the 1982 New York International Film and TV Festival.

**High School Production**

| | |
|---|---|
| *Type:* | Video |
| *Length:* | 30 min. |
| *Source:* | Downtown Community TV Center |
| | 87 LaFayette Street |
| | New York City, NY 10013 |

This video presents five film documentaries produced by high school students, most of whom had dropped out or been kicked out of school before entering "Satellite Academy."

**Living with Parents: Conflicts, Comforts and Insights**

| | |
|---|---|
| *Type:* | Video |
| *Length:* | 45 min. |
| *Cost:* | Purchase $249 |
| *Source:* | Human Relations Media |
| | Room CC |
| | 175 Tompkins Avenue |
| | Pleasantville, NY 10570-9973 |

The video explores conflicts between teenagers and their parents. It talks about the conflicting polarities of wanting to be independent and wanting to be cared for, and looks at ambivalence in parents who may find it hard to let go of their children. The program gives students some specific tactics for improving their relationships with parents.

**Risk-Taking and You**

| | |
|---|---|
| *Type:* | Video |
| *Length:* | 23 min. |
| *Cost:* | Purchase $165 |
| *Title no.:* | CC-842-VS |
| *Source:* | Human Relations Media |
| | Room CC |
| | 175 Tompkins Avenue |
| | Pleasantville, NY 10570-9973 |

The program examines why teenagers are so inclined to take senseless risks and challenges students to explore risk taking in their own lives. Through both real-life interviews with teenage risk takers and compelling dramatizations, the differences between healthy and unhealthy risk taking are clearly illustrated. Advice is given on how to consciously assess a risk.

**School Dropouts:** Parts 1 and 2
*Type:*     Filmstrip with cassette
*Source:*   Prentice-Hall Media
            150 White Plains Road
            Tarrytown, NY 10591

This two-part filmstrip explores the reasons for students' dropping out of school, offers solutions for eliminating the problem, and suggests ways for helping those who have already dropped out. (An Associated Press Special Program.)

**Student Stress: Coping with Academic Pressures**
*Type:*     Video
*Length:*   38 min.
*Cost:*     Purchase $205
*Source:*   Human Relations Media
            Room CC
            175 Tompkins Avenue
            Pleasantville, NY 10570-9973

This video looks at some of the reasons why stress symptoms among young people have increased threefold in the last 15 years. It discusses the physiological nature of stress and shows some stress reduction techniques. Interviews with students show specific causes of stress. Concrete tips for dealing with a variety of stress situations are given.

# Organizations

**National Committee on Youth Suicide Prevention (NCYSP)**
825 Washington Street
Norwood, MA 02062
(617) 769-5986
*Executive Director: Pamela Canter*

A volunteer network working to increase public awareness; publicize warning signals; establish a national information and referral system; acquire, organize, and disseminate current information; and assist in the development of local youth suicide prevention programs. NCYSP encourages federal involvement, maintains a speakers' bureau, sponsors interdisciplinary professional conferences, compiles statistics, and bestows awards.

PUBLICATIONS: *National Directory of Youth Suicide and Intervention Programs,* annual; *Newsletter,* quarterly; *Guide to Resources* (brochure).

**National Listen America Club (NLAC)**
P.O. Box 5005
Westlake Village, CA 91359
(805) 497-9457
*President: Earl J. Labry*

Local group memberships of junior and senior high school students have pledged not to smoke, drink alcohol, or use drugs for the purpose of "getting high." The club provides a variety of community service projects including an annual national two-hour television special. Projects are designed to promote, support, and recognize the positive and constructive things young people are doing.

PUBLICATIONS: *Tune In* (newsletter), biweekly; *Listen America Magazine,* monthly. Convention/meeting annually in summer.

**National Organization of Adolescent Pregnancy and Parenting (NOAPP)**
P.O. Box 2365
Reston, VA 22090
(703) 435-3948
*Coordinator: Sharon Rodine*

Composed of professionals, paraprofessionals, parents, young people, and other concerned individuals, the group's purpose is to provide complete and integrated services designed to prevent and resolve problems associated with adolescent pregnancy and parenthood.

PUBLICATIONS: *Network* (newsletter), quarterly; *Directory of Adolescent Pregnancy and Parenting Programs,* periodic. Annual conference.

**Potsmokers Anonymous (PA)**
316 East Third Street
New York, NY 10009
(212) 254-1777
*Director: Ms. Perry Izenson*

This educational program consists of a nine-week course for
people who want to stop smoking marijuana. It offers
intensive weekend courses for people from outside the
greater New York City area and holds public information
meetings twice a week.

PUBLICATIONS: Newsletter, periodical.

**Special Approaches to Juvenile Assistance (SAJA)**
1352 Q Street, NW, 3d Floor
Washington, DC 20009
(202) 546-7788
*Executive Director: Cornelius S. Williams*

This youth service project provides support and alternatives
for young people in crisis and for their families, helping them
to make choices about their lives. It has sponsored several
projects, including a job-finding cooperative, short- and long-
term group foster homes, a foster placement program, and a
house for runaways. Services include individual, group, and
family counseling; court advocacy; legal, medical, and
psychiatric referrals; job and school placements; tutoring;
housing and moving assistance. It maintains two residential
facilities, one for court-ordered juveniles and the other for
dependent girls. Sponsors annual in-house training sessions,
maintains library, and conducts research.

**Straight, Inc. (Drug Abuse) (SI)**
P.O. Box 21686
St. Petersburg, FL 33742
(813) 576-8929
*Executive Director: Mel J. Riddile*

Composed of trained personnel, adolescent drug users and
their families, and rehabilitated drug users, this group's
objective is to treat drug-using adolescents through the use
of an intensive, highly structured, progressive therapeutic

process, taking 9 to 12 months to complete and involving the drug user and the family. A number of services and programs are available and centers are currently located in 7 locations.

PUBLICATIONS: *Epidemic* (newsletter), periodic; also publishes reprints and produces videotapes.

**Target—Helping Students Cope with Alcohol and Drugs**
P.O. Box 20626
11724 Plaza Circle
Kansas City, MO 64195
(816) 464-5400
*Administrator: Charles Stebbins*

This is a project of the National Federation of State High School Associations that provides information to its membership about helping students deal with drugs and alcohol. It acts as a resource center for information on chemical abuse and prevention through the twelfth grade. It also provides referral service for literature, prevention programs, speakers, and treatment facilities for adolescents and offers workshops and seminars.

PUBLICATIONS: Brochure.

**Teen-Age Assembly of America (TAAA)**
998 Ala Kapua Street
Honolulu, HI 96818
(808) 833-2422
*President: Naomi S. Campbell*

Members of the Assembly are students of elementary and intermediate school, high school, and college. The purpose is to get young people involved in overcoming juvenile delinquency through their own efforts in constructive community activities. It conducts drug panels, conferences, policeteenage relations conferences, the White House Conference on Children and Youth, and Youth Constitutional Convention. The "I Like My School" Project attempts early identification of antisocial behavior among young students. The Youth Against Drugs Project works to prevent drug usage and abuse by teenagers and maintains a national task force on drug prevention in sports.

PUBLICATIONS: *Lynda Byrd Johnson Speaks* and *Teen-Age Assembly Comes of Age.*
Annual convention/meeting. Presently inactive.

**The Youth Project (TYP)**
1555 Connecticut Avenue, NW, Room 501
Washington, DC 20036
(202) 483-0030
*Executive Director: Andrea Kydd*

The project supports democratic, community-oriented change by strengthening community groups that address significant social, political, and economic problems. Founded by young people, most projects to improve the community seek to get the entire community involved. It allocates seed grants to enable organizations to begin operations and refers groups to other sources of funds. It serves in a networking capacity.

PUBLICATIONS: Annual Report; brochure.

Many schools have Big Brother/Big Sister organizations. Being a big brother or big sister to younger people can be just what an older young person needs to gain a strong sense of self-worth and to share experiences that can ease the younger one's adjustments to an often hostile world. In addition, various religious denominations offer a variety of kinds of support, counseling, and real help to those with a wide range of needs for special help.

# Hotlines and Other Help for Substance Abusers

ADPA (Alcohol and Drug Problems Association)
Women's Commission on Alcohol and Drugs
402 Metro Square Building
St. Paul, MN 55101

Alcohol and Drug Abuse Education Program
U.S. Office of Education
400 Maryland Avenue SW
Washington, DC 20202

NarcAnon (for friends, relatives of people with narcotics problems, similar to AlAnon)
(213) 547-5800

Narcotics Anon (similar to Alcoholics Anonymous)
(818) 780-3951

National Cocaine Hotline (24-hour assistance)
(800) COCAINE

National Institute on Drug Abuse (NIDA)
(800) 662-4357

NIDA (gives information to callers about local treatment facilities in their community)
(800) 662-HELP

PRIDE (Parents Resource Institute for Drug Education)
(800) 241-9746

# CHAPTER 6

# Looking to the Future

He did not know what he wanted to do. He had majored in mathematics but could not see himself going on to graduate school. He could not see himself teaching or doing anything. He spent sleepless nights on his narrow bed in his airless room listening to his uncle cough and wondering what to do.

Chaim Potok, *The Book of Lights* (New York: Alfred A. Knopf, 1981), 73.

Long before they lift the tassels of their mortarboards, each one's hand moving the tassel from left to right on graduation night, many of them know what to do, where to go, how to arrive there, who to be—and they've taken the steps they need to focus clearly on the first step toward a larger goal.

But there are also those who, like Gershon Loran in *The Book of Lights*, simply let things happen by chance because they don't define a direction for themselves—don't create a mental image of themselves as they want to be 5, 10, or 25 years from now. When that's the case, some people arbitrarily follow along with whatever their friends are doing or enroll in a trade school or college because somebody else said it was the thing for them to do. Later they look around and wonder how they got where they are and what they can do to get out of it and figure out a direction with real meaning. Not everyone drifts into going to college the way the young man in Potok's novel did, but more are doing it today than was true for young people before World War II. At that time, a smaller percentage of people graduated from high school and even fewer of those went on to college. Most went with a clear goal in mind or because their family tradition and money made it the thing to do.

---

During the post–World War II years, the number of people entering college—many with the financial backing of the GI Bill—rose sharply. Before that time, many high school graduates (if they stayed in school that long) went directly into the workforce—in many cases in a family business or trade—got married, settled, stayed where they were (with periodic pay raises and increasing responsibility if they showed dependability and initiative), and got on with their lives. No big decisions were required because there weren't many options.

But things are more complex these days. In a highly mobile, continuously changing world that offers many attainable choices at nearly any point in a person's lifetime, the problem of choice is quite complicated. A number of elements influence that choice, working to narrow the process systematically, but the availability and range of choices of what to do with the rest of your life is a fairly new phenomenon. And when people fail to make their own choices, they fail to have the feeling of some degree of control over how their lives turn out. Some elements can't be controlled, but taking control over those that can be controlled gives an important sense of progress and meaning to life.

After the post–World War II rush to the colleges, the number enrolling is slightly less. Yet about half of all graduating seniors enroll in either two- or four-year colleges. The following six categories of choices of what to do after graduation offer many more choices within each larger category:

1. Move directly into the workforce
2. Work a few years, then enroll in a vocational school or college
3. Choose a trade or vocational school for specialized training
4. Attend a two-year college for a certificate or degree program, then begin a career or transfer to a four-year college

5. Apply for admission to a four-year college
6. Enlist in a branch of the military service

In choosing one of the six categories, the decision maker picks the one in which advantages outweigh disadvantages. Any decision involves giving something up. For example, when Bill's dad said he wanted Bill to come into the family business as soon as he finished high school, Bill felt secure. He knew the work well and that there'd be no earthshaking adjustments. Yet Bill yearned to strike out on his own, move to another community, test his skills where he wasn't known. Should he choose security and the familiar or risk going into the unknown?

Once the decision is made, it's best not to look back but to move ahead with the necessary planning to make the choice work in the best possible ways. And while the decision of what to do after graduation certainly can determine the level of personal satisfaction a person may or may not realize, the decision is not irreversible. After a fair trial period, if the choice isn't working, then it's time to reevaluate and assess what and how to change direction.

Long before graduation time—as mentioned earlier in this book in "Planning a Course of Study" (page 40)—it's crucial to ask advice from respected sources, seek reliable help, and spy out every possibility in order to make the right choices for the future—not just what to do but where to be and with whom. Help is available in all the places mentioned in earlier parts of this book and in other places, too, including the school guidance office, trusted teachers, peers, books and magazines (magazines and other publications specifically written to the high school and post–high school student give the most current information and advice as well as say it in a useful format), family, respected people in the field the younger person is interested in, experienced professionals in postsecondary training and education, armed services recruiters, and commercial and private counseling/advising services. The most ready source of help is material mailed to high school seniors by various institutions. The information these seniors get gives them some idea of the variety of choices they have and something about each of those choices. These details can guide their readers to cross off some options, mark others to explore, and still others to follow up on as soon as possible.

# Tough Choices

In making that important choice of direction, people need to look at the question from every possible angle. For example, Lynne may fantasize about being the first woman president of the United States (or being a rock star or a famous brain surgeon), but her self-knowledge tells her that she'd find it difficult to cope with any kind of career that would take away her need for privacy. At the same time, she's also very bright and talented. If she sets her sights too low, she'll soon become bored with her life. She'll need to search for something that can suit both sides of her personality; but she'll probably also have to work on learning to be more outgoing and to give up part of her privacy while still protecting as much of it as she needs.

Paul is a strong B student, with quite a few A's scattered in, and especially likes his math classes. But he's enjoyed his art class and working in wood. At first he thought he wanted to go to college to major in accounting and become a Certified Public Accountant. The school counselors encouraged him to choose that as his goal. Yet the more he thought about being tied to a desk and an office, the more Paul resisted that choice. He ended by enrolling in a four-year carpentry apprentice program that incorporated classroom work with on-the-job paid training. He likes working with his hands and being outdoors, free to move and have variety in his tasks. He can see the product of his work taking shape beneath his hands—and still uses his math skills.

Cindy's favorite subject is science—all kinds. She's narrowed a career choice to two major fields: engineering or pharmacy. After thorough research, she decides on pharmacy. The determining reason? She wants to be able to choose where she lives and thinks she'll probably prefer a small community. If she became an engineer, she'd probably have fewer choices of where to live and those choices would primarily be in a city.

Of the twenty careers that will show the most important growth in the next decade, more than half require six months to two or more years of vocational or technical training. The remaining careers require between four and ten years of college education. The careers include jobs in accounting, computers and electronics, engineering, travel agencies, flight attending, health care, legal and paralegal services, cosmetology, food services, lodging management, secretarial services, and pre-school and elementary school teaching. Even the field that requires the shortest training time of six months to a year, cosmetology, demands continuous updating and retraining (*Advance*, 7, 9).

Not everyone can have their first choice. Frequently, compromises have to be made. For example, Steven's family could not spare him to leave home and enroll at the state university, nor could they figure out any way to finance his education there even if they could spare him. So Steven lived at home for his first two years out of high school, worked at a full-time job and contributed to the family budget, and also studied at night at the local community college. Because of his financial need, his classes were paid for in scholarships. By the time he'd completed an associate's degree, his high academic standing earned him a transfer plus full financial help to the university—and his family situation had changed so that it was now possible for him to leave home.

In Robert Cormier's novel, *Beyond the Chocolate War*, Carter, a high school senior, is finding it impossible to overcome the jock image he'd earned as captain of the boxing and football teams. His plans to go to the college he wants seem doomed:

> Carter had gunned for a scholarship but had been unsuccessful. He had not yet even received an acceptance [from the college he'd applied to] . . . nobody saw beyond his jock image. (53)

Unless someone takes a chance on him, Carter will probably have to take a circular route rather than a direct one to reach his goal, such as beginning in a college that will accept him, proving himself, and then reapplying to the one of his choice.

# Choosing a Focus

In deciding on a focus, each individual might begin by making a self-assessment—a list of strengths and weaknesses, interests and talents, personality and character traits, background experiences and influences, values and beliefs, goals and dreams. The assessment provides a base that helps individuals decide what they want in life, why they want it, what's within reach, steps they need to take, obstacles to their goal and how to overcome them, and sources of help. They might also think about different ways to "package" their assets in order to broaden their options.

Whether choosing to go directly into work, post–high school training or schooling, or a branch of the military, careful research of the many choices open in any one of these directions can pay off later in time, energy, a reduced frustration and adjustment level and period, and in a more productive experience. This is the wrong time to be timid or to hold back in asking questions and for advice and help from every possible source. Research means any decision will be an informed decision, not something that happens by chance. The better informed the decision, the better control each individual will have over what happens—and the greater motivation and self-discipline to get where they want to go.

# Focusing on the Choice

## WORK

Whether someone decides to go to work right after high school graduation as a temporary or a permanent step, finding the best possible job is important not only for job satisfaction but for personal satisfaction and future possibilities. At this point, several questions may be asked: What kind of job? Where are the places the job is available? Will a move away from home and/or the community be necessary? Is that an option?

If, for economic or other reasons, the person chooses not to leave the community, other questions arise: What job opportunities are available to high school graduates here? Which ones match the individual's personal traits, interests, and goals as well as background and training? What advantages and disadvantages go with each type of job? Will the work require further training? Does the employer provide on-the-job training and/or instruction? What benefits and wage raises are offered? Are there opportunities to advance? For how long will this job satisfy the applicant's needs? Can it lead to other opportunities? What kinds, how many, where, and how frequently might they be available?

## MILITARY SERVICE

Young people choose to join a branch of the military for a variety of reasons. There are those, of course, who plan to make it a lifetime career. Some decide to try for acceptance to one of the military academies where they can get a top quality education. Their schooling obligates them to a certain number of years of service following their graduation.

Some students want time to look around and see what there is in the world before setting specific life goals. For them the military offers a job with pay, the opportunity to become trained in a field they're interested in, and even the opportunity to take college classes while they're serving, which they can transfer for credit later. If they do decide to take college credit classes, their service branch picks up the tab, thus saving tuition costs. Indeed, saving money is another reason some students join the military—it's a way to get a free college education. Some choose ROTC training for financial help at a traditional university and, in turn, must serve a required number of years in the service following their graduation from the university.

While the reasons to join a branch of the military are many—some want the discipline and the structure of military life—those persons who object to military rules and regulations, the uniforms and restrictions of life on a military base may decide that the benefits are not worth the cost.

# Focusing toward Further
# Training and Education

When people identify a specific or general field of interest for study and/or a career, they need to find out how to qualify for admission to an institution that will train them in that field so as to qualify for a job after graduation. In deciding what to do after graduation from high school, there is a basic question students can ask that can help clarify their direction and goals: Is the purpose for going to school to prepare for earning or is it for learning? Although the emphasis today says school is a means for preparing for a career that can give people the "good life"—i.e., possessions and leisure activities—there are those who say that schooling is a time for intellectual, emotional, social, and moral development and that "job training" can come later. For most people the answer is a blend of the two purposes—to make the school years a time of cultural and intellectual growth from which a career can become something larger than a job, a life work, for which school provides the initial steps. The more years of schooling the person has, the richer life should be—at least in theory.

In today's technology, a high school diploma is the bare minimum number of years of school needed to get a decent job and quality of life. A study titled "The Forgotten Half" analyzed 16–24-year-olds who ended their schooling with a high school diploma. Conducted by the William T. Grant Foundation's Commission on Youth and America's Future in 1988, the study reveals some startling facts:

> In 1986 just 36 percent of male high school graduates found work in "stable, high-wage occupations" compared to 57 percent in 1968, and real wages for all young men dropped 26 percent between 1973 and 1980.

> In 1986 only 22 percent of males under age 20 held manufacturing jobs compared with 44 percent in 1973.

> Most high school graduates can only find work in the lower-paying service jobs and often can get only part-time, low-pay/no-benefits work (4–5).

The need for more training and education following high school graduation is corroborated almost daily by various experts. As long ago as 1970, Kenneth B. Clark wrote that "increasing industrialization and automation of our economy will demand larger numbers of skilled and educated and fewer uneducated workers" (90). Even when people are well into an established career today, they need to continually retrain, return for more schooling, and prepare to use their skills and knowledge in different ways.

## Independence One Step at a Time

Kate had always thought she wanted to go to college. She liked school and was interested in a number of subjects. But she hesitated to go directly from her small town and school to the big state university where most of her friends were going. It was hard not to follow the crowd. But something inside her told her she needed to break away from her dependence on home and family in gradual steps. Kate's self-knowledge helped her make the choice that suited her personality and values.

Her first goal was to learn to live away from home and become independent. To do that, she enrolled in a two-year college just a few hours' drive from home and rented a small apartment near the college. She thought she'd learn a trade or a skill that could get her a job any time or that she could use in other ways later in life. She picked the college's course in horse care and training and soon had a part-time job at a stable in addition to her classes.

After completing her course, she moved to another community and took a job training horses. In two more years, she was offered a position at a local hospital in the personnel department. Her experience with horses, strange as it might seem at first, helped her in working with people. Now Kate began taking some night classes that would count toward a bachelor's degree. She had her feet firmly planted on the ground and felt she'd gained her independence. Soon she resigned from her job at the hospital and enrolled at the state university, ready to meet the challenge there and with a life career goal in mind and skills and experience to fall back on should the need arise.

# Choosing a School with Care

It's important to check the reliability of a training school and wise to visit the school itself and talk personally with school officials, students currently enrolled, and with recent graduates, if possible. A number of trade and vocational schools charge enormous amounts of money but don't give their students the training they need to qualify for jobs they want, nor are they helping students find jobs once they complete the training. Before enrolling in a school, a student needs to be sure of the answers to some questions. What proof does the school offer that they are reputable and that their graduates do well when they leave? And is the training truly focused on the skills the student needs to qualify for his or her career goal? In short, is the person getting a good buy for her money?

Finding the right college involves thorough research. Every source of help gives the person who is searching another piece of the total picture. Yet it's impossible to know everything about every college, so the best thing to do is to identify those elements most important to the individual in getting that college education.

A strong high school counselor can offer invaluable help to the student in any of the six possible categories of choice. Not only can that counselor offer her own expertise and the materials and people available in the school, but she has invaluable information for sources of help outside the school— ones the inexperienced person may not have known about or thought to explore. In addition, the honest recommendation a good counselor can give the student may mean the difference between getting or not getting what he wants—the job, the postsecondary training or education, financial assistance, or the best plan to follow in a branch of the military.

But if a school counselor isn't doing all she can or should, the student should recognize that and do what he needs to do on his own, including getting outside help. Moreover, people shouldn't rely on the counselor to do it all for them. Each person is responsible for getting letters and forms of application done correctly and in on time and for taking the necessary steps at the appropriate times. Asking help from people who are aware of the necessary requirements and procedures is an important part of progressing more smoothly toward a goal.

Among the items a college checklist search might include are:

> The school's reputation in general and particularly in the prospective student's fields of interest
>
> Whether it's public or private, large or medium or small in size, and how it's funded
>
> Geographic location and accessibility
>
> What type of instructors teach lower-division classes (graduate assistants, associate professors, full professors, or others)
>
> Class size (the range might be from 15 to a class to 300)
>
> What the school looks for in its student population as well as in its teaching and support staffs
>
> Total cost of a typical school year and how those costs are broken down
>
> Financial aid available
>
> Admission requirements (highly selective, selective, or open enrollment)
>
> Special programs and services open to freshmen as well as to advanced students
>
> Level of difficulty in transferring
>
> Whether or not graduate study is offered and in what fields
>
> Kinds of housing available
>
> Community opportunities and cultural opportunities offered by the college as well as physical and recreational choices
>
> Any career-connected or exchange study that might be offered
>
> Services available to students in getting advice and help in career choices and placement

Opinions and advice of current and past students at the college

After all the research and paper work, nothing tells so much as an actual visit to a campus. Such a visit, especially when a general and a specific focus is planned, can tell the prospective student whether or not a particular school suits his personality and style, enforces what he believes in, and challenges his intellect appropriately.

In narrowing the choices of schools, a student should include one that seems like an "impossible dream," one that's likely to accept her, and several where she could either be accepted or rejected. One thing the process teaches most people is that rejections happen to nearly everyone, and not necessarily because they're not desirable, promising students. Many elements come into play in a college's decisions of which students to accept and which to turn down. Sometimes being from a different geographic area, belonging to a minority group, or applying for a nontraditional major (women in engineering, men in nurse training), or having an unusual talent can be the factor that admits one student over another. But by applying to several colleges, the chances of being accepted at a place the student has checked on and found at least satisfactory increase, and he can start college on time.

## Application Forms and Letters, Letters of Recommendation, Interviews

Whether a person is planning to enter the workforce, post–high school vocational training or college, a branch of the military, or asking for financial aid, the person will need to fill out forms, possibly write a letter of application, provide one or more letters of recommendation, and be interviewed. These steps in the process of acceptance or rejection provide ways of enlarging the picture of the potential candidate. The candidate, in turn, can learn more about the place to which she's applying and whether she'll fit in or be uncomfortable there.

The applicant wants to make the application letter and form, the letters of recommendation, and the personal interview reveal her as a desirable candidate—one whose application stands out among dozens or hundreds of others. The application form should be filled out exactly as directed and should be neat and easy to read. Any portions that allow for more than a word or phrase response give the candidate an opportunity to reveal personality and character traits or special experiences that could give her an edge in the selection process. It pays off to ask a trusted person to read over the completed form to check for spelling or punctuation errors as well as to ensure that the questions are answered clearly, directly, and completely.

A letter of application or an essay portion of the application form reveals something of the candidate's personality and character, values and goals, and background experiences that would be an asset to the employer, school, or military service. Here's where writing ability is an asset—in more ways than one. Not only can the ability to express information and ideas clearly and interestingly in writing win the writer what she's applying for, but that ability is an important asset to the place that accepts her. It's important in such a letter or essay to present one's self honestly—not to be someone different in order to impress the readers. Even if that means a rejection rather than an acceptance, in the long run the rejection will be for the best because an acceptance could result in a "bad match" between student and college—and a bad college experience. It always helps to keep in mind who will be reading the letter and what they'll be looking for, the purpose of the letter, and the context in which it will be read and considered.

Most employers, postsecondary schools, financial aid offices, and branches of the military ask their applicants for letters of recommendation. Choosing the right people to write those letters can mean the difference between being accepted and being rejected. Three guidelines will help in getting the right letters of recommendation:

1. The letter should be written by someone who knows the candidate well and who has had a positive relationship with the candidate. These writers should know the candidate in ways that reveal the person's

quality of character and personality traits, the candidate's special skills and knowledge, and/or any special experiences that have had a significant impact to strengthen the person's life.

2. The person writing the letter should be an effective writer. He or she is also creating an impression of the candidate, and if the letter is carelessly done or presents no helpful information, the result is a strike against the applicant.

3. The letter writer should know specifically what kinds of details the letter should include. It's up to the applicant to let that person know exactly what the letter should contain, to whom it should be addressed, and the deadline date for it to mailed.

It's common courtesy to supply the person writing a recommendation with a stamped, correctly addressed envelope. It's probably best for the person writing to use his or her own letterhead stationery. Again, this depends on what the directions are. Because the person writing the letter is probably taking time and care from a busy schedule, it's important for the one doing the requesting to show appreciation both personally and with a written thank-you note.

The personal interview, like the letter of application or essay, is another way of enlarging the picture the candidate presents, as well as enlarging the one being given to the candidate by the employer or institution. It's another way to find out whether this would be a positive match. A practice interview with a friend, teacher, or relative can prepare the person being interviewed for possible questions. She can think ahead of time how to answer them as well as alleviate some of the natural nervousness that goes along with being interviewed. It is also prudent to take along a list of questions to ask that let the interviewer know the candidate has done her homework.

For a job interview, it's wise to find out all the information possible about the position being applied for before going, in order to save time and give a favorable impression. And of course the usual rules of being rested, alert, neatly and appropriately dressed, and demonstrating an upbeat attitude about being interviewed all apply.

The letter of application or essay and the interview can be used to explain or to include what a form fails to show about a candidate. For example, Stuart could explain that he took only one advanced placement course and no foreign language in high school because the school offered only a limited curriculum and the only two advanced placement courses fell during the same class period, allowing him to take only one. He could add that he's been studying Spanish on his own by checking out lessons and tapes on interlibrary loan and by making friends with a Spanish-speaking neighbor who spent several evenings a week talking with him in Spanish. This information tells the interviewer that Stuart has made the best of what was available to him, and also that he was enterprising enough to tackle a foreign language on his own and had the determination to stick with it.

If a person is rejected by the college she had her heart set on, she can keep trying. For example, she might first write to ask the office of admissions to make sure an error hadn't been made or to explain where her application was deficient. She might volunteer to make up any classes required for admission during the summer term or in some other way. (Some colleges offer "catch-up" classes during the academic year.) If the weaknesses are not academic, an applicant can explain how those weaknesses might be compensated for or strengthened.

Sometimes a student isn't admitted to the college within the university she wants (for example, the college of engineering) but can be admitted to another one (the school of business). If she accepts that and makes high marks, she can reapply for the college of engineering and have a good chance of being accepted. The same approach can work by enrolling in another university and then reapplying to the university of her first choice. Persistence pays.

## Tests

While most employers probably won't ask for a high school student's SAT (Scholastic Aptitude Test) or ACT (American

College Testing Program) scores or even for achievement scores, they will want to know how well the person did in the classes that relate to skills and knowledge needed in the job. They also want to know how often the student missed or was late to classes. The classes the student took as electives also indicate strong personal and job-related interests, as do the choices of outside activities and any volunteer or paid work experiences. Career aptitude and interest tests may be useful.

As the chapter on planning pointed out, students need to know whether the postsecondary institutions they want require any tests for consideration in the application process and which ones. It's a waste of time and money to take the wrong ones and be denied admission. Not all postsecondary institutions place the same weight on test scores as an admissions requirement, so the student needs to find out about that, too. Some schools care primarily that the student has taken the recommended core of classes, while others demand disciplined and rigorous test preparation for the student to be admitted.

# Matters of Money

No one doubts the high cost of advanced training and education. Most families need at least some financial help to send their high school graduate for more schooling. It pays to be a smart shopper in finding the best buy for the money in a college, as in purchasing a home or an automobile. Some schools give more value per dollar than others. Here again, materials sent to students in high school provide a wealth of information and a starting point. These materials also include information about grants, loans, work-study, and scholarships.

Money to help students get their education can come from many sources, so it's wise to search out as many as possible. At the school level, the school guidance office schedules times when parents and students can meet to learn about financial aid. Parents are asked to fill out the required financial statement if they want their student to be considered for scholarship awards.

Many local scholarships offered by various clubs, foundations, professions, businesses, and industries are the ones students tend to try for first. And people don't have to be at the top of the class or at the poverty level to qualify. Other factors are considered, an important one being whether the selection committee believes this student stands a strong chance of completing his program of study.

Besides local sources, aid can come from the college or vocational school that has accepted the student—especially if that person shows a strong talent or interest in a particular subject. So people need to research both the high school and the college financial aid offices.

As mentioned earlier, the Reserve Officers' Training Corps program (ROTC) pays the student's way but also asks for years of service in return. A number of government loans, grants, and scholarships are also available.

If a student has won prizes at science fairs, for example, chances are good she'll get a scholarship from some business or industry in that field. The National Merit Scholarship is something many students across the nation test for, too.

Many people end up using a combination of financial support. For example, Donald gets a sizable scholarship from a large corporation, a smaller one from a local service club, and a work-study plan from the college he'll attend. The combination will pay all his expenses. If part of the aid is in the form of a loan, the borrower is expected to repay within the time specified. Since learning to manage money wisely is part of becoming an adult, this can be a worthwhile learning experience.

Bookstores, libraries, university and college financial aid offices and libraries, high school guidance offices, private advisors, and computer software searches are among the possible sources of help in addition to the advice from former students, teachers, people in the careers the student is interested in, friends, and other family members.

Generally people are advised to pick the college they want first and worry about the money it takes afterward. In most cases, help is available for the person who truly wants to get an education at a certain institution and has been admitted there. The motto here is to aim high. If a compromise must be made, at least the person knows he's tried his best and then will make the most of what he can get.

# Stepping into the Future

Once a graduate has chosen a direction and is about to follow it—be it a job, marriage, the military, or some institution of higher training and/or education—a whole new life lies ahead. It's both exciting and frightening. But it's important to remind oneself that the new life is not beginning from zero—rather, there are all the growing-up years of experience and learning, an individual's special set of interests and skills and talents, a strong desire to succeed, a support system, and many sources to call on for help.

Whatever happens next is the next chapter of that person's education. As educator John Goodlad said, "Education, then, is a process of individual becoming" (38).

## REFERENCES

*Advance.* Kansas City, MO: Target Marketing, Inc., 1986. 7, 9.

Clark, Kenneth B. "Alternative Schools." *High School 1980.* Ed. by Alvin C. Eurich et al. New York: Pitman Publishing Corporation, 1970.

Cormier, Robert. *Beyond the Chocolate War.* New York: Dell Publishing, 1985.

"The Forgotten Half." Prepared by William T. Grant Foundation's Commission on Youth and America's Future. *Council-Grams,* Urbana, IL (September 1988): 4–5.

Goodlad, John. *What Schools Are For.* Bloomington, IN: Phi Delta Kappa Educational Foundation, 1979.

Potok, Chaim. *The Book of Lights.* New York: Alfred A. Knopf, 1981.

# Resources

## Fiction

Asher, Sandy. **Everything Is Not Enough.** New York: Dell Publishing, 1988. 155p.

Michael's family expects him to enroll in business college after he graduates from high school, and then join his father in his business. Because he doesn't want to disappoint his loving family, Michael is struggling with telling them he doesn't want to major in business; what he wants is to study psychology and use his knowledge to help those who need help. Then he meets Linda, whose personality is very different from his own and who has the courage to follow her dreams. Predominant themes in the novel are self-identity and making wise choices.

Benard, Robert. **A Catholic Education.** New York: Dell Publishing, 1987 [1982]. 276p.

Set in the early sixties, the novel tells the story of Nick Manion's journey toward self-identity over a four-year time span—his last three years of high school and the first year after graduation. Living in a male-dominated world, Nick believes he has a calling to be a Jesuit priest. But at seminary his intensified personal and spiritual journeys bring him into conflicts when "his life-long trust in the fixed order of the universe" falls apart.

Girion, Barbara. **In the Middle of a Rainbow.** New York: Charles Scribner's Sons, 1983. 197p.

Corrie has always been a model student and daughter. Working to save money for college and getting a scholarship haven't left her much time for fun. So when she begins a romance with a rich and popular athlete, her world brightens considerably. But Todd's wealth creates problems between them, makes her question her values, and almost makes her pass up the chance to go to an East Coast university.

Naylor, Phyllis Reynolds. **The Year of the Gopher.** New York: Bantam Books, 1988. 201p.

When George decides not to go to college but instead spend time finding out what he wants to do, he both shocks and angers his family. His decision is a painful one, not only because of his family's reaction, but also because the kind of jobs he's forced to take are "gopher" (go-fer this, go-fer that) jobs. Still, he does gain a sense of independence. He also learns something about sexual relationships, another aspect of becoming an adult, and handles this part of his learning in a mature way.

Potok, Chaim. **The Book of Lights.** New York: Alfred A. Knopf, 1981. 370p.

Young Gershon Loran, reared by an aunt and uncle and sent to parochial schools and college, has adopted the attitude of staying in the background, going where he's told, and doing what he's told simply because he doesn't really know what he wants to do with his life, except maybe to keep peace. When the Korean war erupts, Gershon is sent as a chaplain to this land where Judaism has never existed. His friendship with a seminary friend now also in the service (whose father helped develop the atomic bomb), combined with other experiences, at last makes him focus on what meaning his life has.

Strasser, Todd. **Wildlife.** New York: Delacorte, 1987. 180p.

This novel is the final book in Strasser's trilogy detailing the rise and fall of a rock band and its star, Gary Specter. This volume reveals the struggles to keep the band together and how they fail. Strasser shows the grind and emptiness behind the outward glamour of stardom as well as dramatizes the first years after high school graduation in real-life terms.

Tesich, Steve. **Summer Crossing.** New York: Random House, 1982. 373p.

Summer following high school graduation for Daniel Price becomes a series of traumatic experiences. His father is dying of cancer; his relationships with his closest buddies begin changing as each one searches for his own future direction; he discovers a secret about his parents' relationship; and his own first love affair is a strange and frustrating one. With these experiences of death, various kinds of loss, and self-discovery, Daniel matures during the brief summer months.

Thompson, Julian F. **Simon Pure.** New York: Scholastic, 1987. 329p.

Simon Storm is the 15-year-old narrator of this intriguing story of his life just after he enrolls as a freshman at Riddle University. Through Simon's eyes, the reader experiences a variety of events ranging from first love to an attempt to overthrow the university's administration. The complex plot and writing style make the book appropriate for more sophisticated readers.

Van Leeuwen, Jean. **Seems Like This Road Goes On Forever.** New York: Dial Press, 1979. 192p.

Mary Alice's father, a preacher, and her mother, who is totally wrapped up in church activities, are extraordinarily strict with Mary and insist she attend a religiously supported college. But Mary Alice rebels.

Voigt, Cynthia. **Tell Me If the Lovers Are Losers.** New York: Atheneum, 1982. 241p.

Three very different female freshmen at an exclusive college in the early sixties become roommates. Their values conflict, sharpen, then temper as they live and work together and become part of an unbeatable volleyball team. The novel's theme is that of the search for truth.

# Nonfiction

Beatty, Richard H. **The Complete Job Search Book.** New York: John Wiley & Sons, 1988. 236p, index.

This book offers practical applications and a complete approach to the process of seeking suitable employment. The book begins with how to define job objectives, and then follow through the steps in the process of finding and getting a job. The book also includes descriptions of how to prepare several types of resumes as well as appropriate writing style for each type. It describes employment sources and how to use each type; how to use a direct mail campaign in a job search; techniques for effective interviewing and how to negotiate to get an appropriate salary, work schedule, and related elements, including moving costs. The final portion deals with strategies for selecting the right employer.

Birnbach, Lisa. **College Book.** New York: Ballantine, 1984. 509p.

Also the author of The Official Preppy Handbook, Birnbach lists the colleges by states and schools, describing each in a way that captures its individual personality. Designed for the teenage reader, the book's chapters include topics such as the importance of having money, qualities to look for in a roommate, a comparison of high school versus college, how to deal with parents, the best and the worst in everything from bars to bookstores at each college, drugs, religion, and sororities and fraternities.

Blyskal, Jeff, and Marie Hodge. **Reader's Digest College Guide.** Pleasantville, NY: The Reader's Digest Association, Inc., 1988. 23p.

This useful guide is available free from most high school guidance offices or may be ordered at a cost of $1 each from Reprint Editor, Reader's Digest, Pleasantville, NY 10570, or call (914) 241-5374. Quick and easy to read yet thorough and complete, the pamphlet makes a good starting point for the high school student considering entering college after graduation.

Bolles, Richard Nelson. **The 1989 What Color Is Your Parachute?** Berkeley, CA: Ten Speed Press, 1989. 388p, a 199p index, and four appendixes.

This guide is a practical manual for job-hunters and career changers. Bolles's companion book *The Three Boxes of Life* makes a good supplement as it deals with the learning, working, and leisure parts of a daily, weekly, and yearly schedule. Among the specific topics he details in *Parachute* are job hunting and dealing with the shock of various kinds of rejection.

Branscomb, H., O. Milton, J. Richardson, and H. Spivey. **The Competent College Student.** Nashville: Tennessee Higher Education Commission, 1977.

This essay on the objectives and quality of higher education suggests competencies for the college entrant, minimum competencies college students should attain, and desired outcomes for a liberal education.

Chronicle Guidance Publications, Inc. Catalogs available from C.G.P., Inc., Aurora Street, P.O. Box 1190, Moravia, NY 13118-1190; toll-free order line (800) 622-7284.

Offering career guidance materials in print and in video, the C-LECT® jr. program is a career exploration and self-assessment program using workbooks to do inventories of individuals' temperaments and interests. The results of the inventories are scored to see how much formal education an individual needs to enter the world of work. Using the computer, students can enter data and learn career options within particular fields of interest. Some of the topics the Career Profile Guide includes for each occupation on their list are descriptions of the work performed, education and training needed, qualifications to get the job, salary outlook, occupational outlook, related occupations, and other sources of information. Students might ask guidance counselors or teachers to order these or similar materials to aid in their career decisions.

Coburn, Karen Levin, and Madge Lawrence Treeger. **Letting Go: Parents Guide to Today's College Experience.** Bethesda, MD: Adler & Adler, 1988. 283p, bibliography.

Potential college students will want their parents to read this book. The authors point out that what seems to be the end is really a beginning. They tell parents what to expect their college students will experience, beginning with the freshman year and ending with graduation. They offer advice on how to help them reach independence and discuss how college life today has changed from college life a generation ago.

College Research Group. **The Right College—1990.** New York: Arco, 1988. 1,446p, index of majors, general index.

Besides listing and describing 1,500 U.S. and Canadian colleges and universities, the guide tells readers how to use the book, gives a college data table to show information at a glance, discusses choosing and applying for admission to college, and describes the financial aid process.

Duffy, James P. **Cutting College Costs.** New York: Duffy, 1988. 226p.

Duffy outlines strategies for reducing the expense involved in earning a college degree.

Edelhart, Mike. **Breaking through the Job Barrier.** Garden City, NY: Anchor Books/Doubleday, 1981. 224p.

An assortment of real-life job success stories show that the steps to a career aren't always neatly laid out and that breaking in to many fields can be tough. Careers begin, says the author, with personalities. The best way to learn about anything is to observe and talk with the best practitioner in the field. Edelhart observes that some people struggle toward success while others are born to it, but that all who succeed share the common attitude that they knew when they were on their way to achieving it.

Fiske, Edward B. **The Fiske Guide to Colleges.** New York: TIMES Books, 1989. 759p.

A fully updated and expanded edition of Fiske's guide to 291 of the finest public and private colleges in the United States is based on a survey of thousands of students and administrators. The descriptions of what's best and most interesting about individual colleges should help students select the one that's right for them. Written in a candid and lively style, the book answers the questions in the minds of both students and parents on every aspect of life at college.

Fitzgibbon, Dan. **All About Your Money.** New York: Atheneum, 1984. 135p.

The author writes in a readable style about the basic things young people need to know about money, including how to get it, where and why to spend it, and what to do about the "allowance system." He also explains how to get a Social Security card, gives hints about applying for a job, warns of the dangers in borrowing money, and provides insights concerning how to view money.

Fry, Ronald W. **Your First Resume.** Hawthorne, NJ: The Career Press, 1988. (May be ordered from P.O. Box 34, Hawthorne, NJ 07507; (800) CAREER or in NJ, (201) 427-0229. $11.95 postpaid.)

For high school and college students facing decisions, the author of this book recommends they prepare carefully using a logical sequence: begin with the right attitude, find the right match of job or school, try something out before accepting it, write resumes and query letters correctly, and accept an offer or decline it correctly. The author points out that 85 percent of all job opportunities are never announced publicly and that that fact is important for job seekers to know.

**The GIS Guide to Four Year Colleges, 1989.** By the editors of the Guidance Information System. Boston: Houghton Mifflin, 1988. 630p.

Besides the expected data base, this guide features a selection system designed to match students' personal preferences with appropriate colleges.

Greene, Howard, and Robert Minton. **Scaling the Ivy Wall: Twelve Winning Steps to College Admission.** Boston: Little, Brown, 1987. 252p, two appendixes, and worksheets.

The title tells the content of this book for students who hope to win admission to one of the highly competitive Ivy League schools.

Griffith, Susan, et al. **Work Your Way around the World.** Oxford: Vacation Work, 1989. 404p with index and section of useful foreign phrases.

This guidebook lists categories of jobs—such as tourism, agriculture, teaching English, domestic work, business and industry, archaeology, conservation, voluntary workcamps—that allow would-be travelers to explore other countries by working there.

Lang, Larry R., and Thomas H. Gillespie. **Strategy for Personal Finance.** New York: McGraw-Hill Book Co., 1977.

This text provides complete information for personal and financial planning. It includes the process of setting goals, describes how jobs are classified, and points to the need for understanding job trends and personal factors. Financial topics include setting up and keeping records, obtaining safety deposit boxes, personal budgeting, using banking services effectively, obtaining credit, understanding consumerism, providing for transportation (automobile), selecting consumer durables, making housing decisions, safeguarding resources, and building for the future.

Lewan, Lloyd S., with Ronald G. Billingsley, Ph.D. **Women in the Workplace: A Man's Perspective.** Denver, CO: Remington Press, 1988. 95p, bibliography.

According to the authors, "Differences between men and women are not good or bad, but essential, appropriate, and complementary." On this premise they elaborate on the fact that work takes up one-third of a person's life, the importance of personal development for inner peace and a sense of personal worth, and the need to develop relationships.

Morgan, Tom. **Money, Money, Money: How To Get It and Keep It.** Illustrated by Joe Ciardiello. New York: G. P. Putnam's Sons, 1978.

This book provides basic knowledge about money, including how to make it grow and how easily you can lose it. Entertaining narratives provide illustrations of how money can be used and misused.

The National Association of College Admission Counselors (NACAC) provides useful tools that include:

> **A Guide to the College Admission Process** for high school students who plan to continue their education. The 32-page guide gives a step-by-step approach to admission, including definitions of terms and a planning guide. $2/copy.
>
> **NACAC Map of Two- and Four-Year Colleges.** The 25" x 30" two-sided map identifies more than 2,800 U.S. institutions, shows the interstate highway system, and gives a state by state index of colleges and universities. $2/map.
>
> **High School Planning for College-Bound Athletes.** The 16-page booklet opens with a thought-provoking introduction by Penn State football coach Joe Paterno and offers sound advice to athletes preparing for college admission. $2/copy.

Interested persons may send payment or purchase order to NACAC Publications Department, Suite 430, 1800 Diagonal Road, Alexandria, VA 22314. Orders under $10 should be accompanied by payment. Quantity rates given on request.

Schmidt, Peggy J. **Making It on Your First Job.** New York: Avon, 1981. 243p, sources, index.

This comprehensive and easy-to-refer-to guide is intended for young, inexperienced, and ambitious persons. The book provides a complete guide to preparing for a job—including academics, extracurriculars, and internships that get you the job you want; employers, campaigning to get a job, the interview, the first job, bosses, office politics, coworkers, ethics, discrimination, and moving on.

Shields, Charles J. **How To Help Your Teenager Find the Right Career.** New York: The College Board, 1988. 203p.

College and career counselor Shields outlines the process of exploring and choosing a career. He focuses on the wide range of career possibilities and emphasizes the value of self-awareness and the importance of academic and professional preparation. He suggests practical strategies for parents in assisting and in motivating their teenagers, his informed approach enabling families to avoid costly mistakes when making this important decision.

Other helpful books from the College Board include: *College Bound: The Student's Handbook for Getting Ready, Moving In, and Succeeding on Campus* by Evelyn Kaye and Janet Gardner; *How to Pay for Your Children's College Education* by Gerald Krefetz; *The College Guide for Parents* by Charles J. Shields; *Campus Visits and College Interviews* by Zola Dincin Schneider; *Your College Application* by Scott Gelband et al.; *Index of Majors*, the 1988–1989 eleventh edition. For a catalog of publications by this group write to The College Board, 45 Columbus Avenue, New York, NY 10023-6992.

**The Student Guide.** U.S. Department of Education. Washington, DC: U.S. Government Printing Office, 1989.

This complete guide to grants, loans, and work-study financial aid for students provides both general and specific information as well as a definition of terms. High school guidance offices generally make the current issue of this publication available to students.

# Nonprint Materials

**Almos' a Man**
*Type:*     16mm film, color
*Length:*   39 min.

*Cost:*     Rental $13
*Title no.:*  8-0106
*Source:*   Learning Resources Service
          Southern Illinois University at Carbondale
          Carbondale, IL 62901
*Date:*     1976

LeVar Burton, who starred in the popular *Roots,* plays David, a black teenage farm worker in the Deep South who is struggling for a new identity, that of a man, during the late 1930s. (From the American Short Story Series.)

### The Art of Learning
*Type:*     Series of videos
*Length:*   20 min. each video
*Source:*   Great Plains Instructional TV Library
          University of Nebraska
          P.O. Box 80669
          Lincoln, NE 68501
*Date:*     1984

The series includes these topics: "The College Classroom," "The Efficient Learner," "Getting the Message," "Test Taking," "Using the Library," and "The Written Word." Appropriate for postsecondary students.

### Best of Careertrack
*Type:*     Video
*Length:*   Vol. 1, 75 min. S 01928
          Vol. 2, 85 min. S 01929
*Cost:*     Purchase $59.95 each volume; $109.90 the set
*Source:*   University of Illinois Film/Video Center
          1325 South Oak Street
          Champaign, IL 61820

This sampling of excerpts from a popular seminar series includes in Volume 1: delegation of work, setting goals, dealing with difficult people, exceptional customer service, image and self-projection for women, and achieving excellence; and in Volume 2: using assertiveness effectively, stress management, getting results with people power communication, and presentations that win approval.

**Bridges**

*Type:*     16mm film
*Cost:*     Free; borrower pays return postage
*Source:*   Modern Talking Picture Service
            Film Scheduling Center
            5000 Park Street, North
            St. Petersburg, FL 33709
*Date:*     1975

Produced by the American Red Cross, the film presents the story of teenagers who become volunteers with the American Red Cross in order to build bridges of communication and caring into other peoples' worlds. Three case studies deal with the problems of the elderly, the handicapped, and disaster victims.

**Career Hunter: Getting Hired and Advancing**

*Type:*       Video
*Length:*     30 min.
*Cost:*       Purchase $24.95
*Title no.:*  S 02270
*Source:*     University of Illinois Film/Video Center
              1325 South Oak Street
              Champaign, IL 61820

Professionals share the secrets of successful career hunting—the do's and don'ts critical to the search, interview, and promotion after getting hired. Also includes how to build confidence, the 23 things to do to improve the chances for hiring or promotion, how to learn what to expect, and what qualities an employer looks for in a new employee.

**College Explorer**

*Type:*        Microcomputer software; one disk for IBM/PC,
               two disks for Apple
*Cost:*        Purchase $49.95
*Title nos.:*  003187, ISBN 0-874470318-7 (Apple II family);
               003195, ISBN 0-87447-319-5 (IBM PC/XT/AT,
               100 percent compatibles)
*Source:*      The College Board
               45 Columbus Avenue
               New York City, NY 10023-6992
*Date:*        1988

This college-search software allows users to explore a comprehensive and up-to-date data base of information on 2,800 two- and four-year colleges. It includes topics such as majors, enrollment, location, admissions selectivity, and student activities. Special features of the software let the student prioritize the search and sort college lists on the basis of such criteria as size of enrollment and college costs.

### Consumer Reports: Cars . . .

| | |
|---|---|
| *Type:* | Video |
| *Length:* | 50 min. |
| *Cost:* | Purchase $19.95 |
| *Title no.:* | S 00761 |
| *Source:* | University of Illinois Film/Video Center |
| | 1325 South Oak Street |
| | Champaign, IL 61820 |

Subtitled "How to Buy a New or Used Car and Keep It Running Almost Forever," this video is organized into seven segments covering service comparisons, test drives, car loans and insurance, maintenance, and symptoms of trouble spots, and gives consumer advice on selection and hints on maintenance.

### Did You Get My Message?

| | |
|---|---|
| *Type:* | Video |
| *Length:* | 14 min. |
| *Cost:* | Purchase $84.95 |
| *Title no.:* | ES-807 |
| *Source:* | RMI Media Productions |
| | 2807 West 47th Street |
| | Shawnee Mission, KS 66205 |

This live-action video describes how important the effect of verbal and nonverbal communication can be, emphasizing that nonverbal communication creates the first impression a person makes on others. Discusses correct grammar, manners, and tips for effective verbal communication and provides ways of communicating positively to an employer through speech and actions.

### Got a Job Interview?

| | |
|---|---|
| *Type:* | Video |

Length:    28 min.
Cost:      Purchase $185
Title no.: CC-3430-VS
Source:    Human Relations Media
           Room CC
           175 Tompkins Avenue
           Pleasantville, NY 10570-0073

Appropriate for grades 9 through college, the video uses the
example of four young applicants on their first entry-level
job interviews, showing viewers that by learning the requisite
skills, they can turn any job interview into a valuable
learning experience and maximize their chances for success.
It encourages teens to seize every interview opportunity,
recognizing that not every interview leads to a job. It notes
that a positive attitude is the number one job qualification,
shows how to prepare for the interview, illustrates the kinds
of questions that may be asked, and involves viewers in
provocative discussion questions.

**How the Automobile Works**
Type:      Video
Length:    28 min.
Cost:      Purchase $29.95
Title no.: S 00004
Source:    University of Illinois Film/ Video Center
           1325 South Oak Street
           Champaign, IL 61820

Taking the approach that a car is not the enemy, the video
shows viewers about the workings of a car. It helps them
understand and solve many of the problems that may arise,
so they'll feel more confident and enjoy driving more.

**Paying for College**
Type:      Video in VHS, 3/4", and Beta formats
Length:    18 min.
Cost:      Purchase $40
Source:    College Board Film Library
           c/o West Glen Communications, Inc.
           1430 Broadway
           New York, NY 10018
Date:      1985

This production gives students and parents a basic introduction to financial aid and an overview of the financial aid process, covering types and sources of aid, how eligibility is determined, and application procedures. It also makes suggestions for cutting costs and finding alternative sources of financial help.

**Self-Image and Your Career**

| | |
|---|---|
| *Type:* | Video |
| *Length:* | 37 min. |
| *Cost:* | Purchase $205 |
| *Source:* | Human Relations Media |
| | Room CC |
| | 175 Tompkins Avenue |
| | Pleasantville, NY 10570-9973 |

The presentation shows young people why the key to good career decision making is a clear positive self-image. It helps them learn more about themselves—their personality types, aptitudes, life skills, and values—in order to clarify their self-image and use the information as a blueprint for future career choices. It demonstrates that as their self-image grows clearer and stronger, they will find more to like in themselves, have a wider choice of career options, and a greater chance for job success and satisfaction.

**Who Am I and Where Do I Want To Go?**

| | |
|---|---|
| *Type:* | 3/4″ or 1/2″ video |
| *Source:* | Cambridge, The Adult Education Co. |
| | 88 Seventh Avenue |
| | New York, NY 10106 |

The video identifies those abilities, interests, values, personal characteristics, and experiences that have important implications for choosing a job and/or career. (From the Employability Skills Series.)

# Organizations

**American Association for Higher Education (AAHE)**
One Dupont Circle, NW, Suite 600
Washington, DC 20036
(202) 293-6440

*President: Russell Edgerton*

An organization for all segments of postsecondary education, including students, this group seeks to clarify and help resolve critical issues in postsecondary education through conferences, publications, and special projects.

PUBLICATIONS: *AAHE Bulletin*, 10/year; *Change Magazine*, 6/year; also publishes books and reports developed from special projects.


## American Association of Community and Junior Colleges (AACJA)

One Dupont Circle, NW, Suite 410
Washington, DC 10036
(202) 293-7050
*President: Dr. Dale Parnell*

The association's Office of Federal Relations monitors federal education programming and legislation. The organization maintains a library of community, technical, and junior college catalogs, reference books, texts, and journals. Compiles statistics through collected data.

PUBLICATIONS: *AACJA Letter*, weekly; *Community, Technical, and Junior College Journal*, bimonthly; annual directory; statistical directory of two-year colleges; and books, pamphlets for faculty and administrators.


## American Board of Vocational Experts (ABVE)

300 25th Avenue, N, Suite 100N
Physicians' Park B
Nashville, TN 37203
(615) 327-2984
*Executive Officer: Claude Peacock*

The organization promotes uniform high standards of professional practice among vocational consultants. It established the American College of Vocational Experts to develop a professional training academy in vocational studies.

PUBLICATIONS: *Vocational Expert*, periodic. Holds annual convention/meeting.

## American Council on Education (ACE)
One Dupont Circle
Washington, DC 20036
(202) 939-9300
*President: Robert H. Atwell*

The council of colleges and universities, educational organizations, and affiliates represents accredited post-secondary institutions and acts as an advocate on their behalf before Congress, the federal government, and federal and state courts. As an advocate for adult education, the group advances education and teaching methods and services. It nationally administers the GED high school equivalency exam and provides college credit equivalency evaluations for courses taught outside the traditional campus classroom by corporations and the military. It operates a library of 5,000 volumes on higher education and administration.

PUBLICATIONS: *Higher Education and National Affairs,* biweekly; *Education Record,* quarterly; also publishes *A Fact Book on Higher Education,* and publishes and/or distributes yearbooks and directories of institutions of higher education in the United States. Annual convention/meeting.

## Campus Outreach Opportunity League (Youth) (COOL)
810 18th Street, Suite 705
Washington, DC 20006
(202) 783-8855
*Executive Officer: Wayne Meisel*

The League conducts outreach activities involving under-graduate college students in community improvement projects on a volunteer basis. Periodic convention/meeting.

## Community Careers Resource Center (CCRC)
1319 18th Street, NW
Washington, DC 20036
(202) 659-5627
*Administrator: David Guttchen*

The center publishes *Community Jobs,* a monthly nation-wide listing of job and internship opportunities in public interest and community-oriented nonprofit organizations. Provides speakers' bureau for colleges on alternative and socially responsible career options.

PUBLICATIONS (in addition to *Community Jobs*): Reprints on technical assistance, such as *Nonprofits Enter the Computer Age, Survival Planning for the 80's: Fundraising Strategies for Grassroots Organizations*, and *Making the Community Your Career.*

**National Association of Industrial Technology (NAIT)**
204 A Sill Hall
Eastern Michigan University
Ypsilanti, MI 48197
(313) 487-0358
*Executive Director: Alvin E. Rudisill*

Composed of industrial organizations, administrators, industrialists, educators, students, and graduates of industrial technology programs, the group provides opportunities for collecting, developing, and disseminating information concerning industrial technology education. It promotes research related to the curricula of industrial technology and acts as an accrediting agency for baccalaureate level technology programs. It also bestows awards and compiles statistics.

PUBLICATIONS: *Journal of Industrial Technology*, quarterly; *Conference Proceedings*, annual; *Program Directory*, annual; also publishes committee handbook and research monographs. Annual conference with exhibits.

**U.S. Association of Evening Students (USAES)**
c/o Alta High
510 North Avenue
Weston, VA 02193
(617) 899-3183
*President: Anthony Farma*

The group includes representatives of evening, adult, and part-time college and university student governments and affiliate members who are students from institutions without student government organizations. Its goal is to enhance the education of evening students. The organization encourages and develops student leadership, conducts legislative workshops, and provides scholarships. It also bestows awards and maintains biographical archives.

PUBLICATIONS: *Guidebook for Evening Student Governments,* irregularly. It is affiliated with the National University of Continuing Education Association and holds a semiannual convention/meeting.

# Military Services

Persons interested in contacting their nearest representative of a branch of the military may consult the telephone directory listings under United States Government. Public and school libraries usually have *The National Directory of Addresses and Telephone Numbers* in the reference section where government and other numbers of national interest may be located. Some national addresses and/or telephone numbers include:

U.S. Air Force Academy
Office of Admissions
HQ USAFA/RRS
Colorado Springs, CO 80840-5651
(303) 472-2520

Department of the Air Force
Pentagon Room 5C931
Washington, DC 20330-0000
(202) 697-4100

Army National Guard
P.O. Box 6000
Clifton, NJ 07015

Department of the Army
HQ, U.S. Army Recruiting Command
P.O. Box 7721
Clifton, NJ 07015-0118

Director of Admissions
U.S. Coast Guard Academy
New London, CT 06320-4195
(203) 444-8501

U.S. Marine Corps Headquarters
Washington, DC 20380-0000
(202) 694-4080
FAX: (914) 938-3828

Director of Admissions
U.S. Merchant Marine Academy
Kings Point, NY 11024
(516) 482-8200
Toll-free outside NY (800) 732-6267

Director of Admissions
U.S. Military Academy
West Point, NY 10996-1797
(914) 938-4041
FAX: (914) 938-3828

Director of Candidate Guidance
U.S. Naval Academy
Annapolis, MD 21402-5018
(800) 638-9156
(301) 267-4361

NROTC (for college scholarships and officer training)
Navy Opportunity Information Center
P.O. Box 5000
Clifton, NJ 07015-9939
(800) 327-NAVY

People interested in other military Reserve Officers' Training Corps programs should inquire about the ones offered by the colleges and universities of their choice.

# Index

WITHDRAWN
103 '2023
SAINT LOUIS UNIVERSITY